# Voices in the Wilderness

*Contemporary Wildlife Writings*

# Voices in the Wilderness

*Contemporary Wildlife Writings*

*Edited by*
Prerna Singh Bindra

Rupa . Co

Published 2010 by
**Rupa Publications India Pvt. Ltd.**
7/16, Ansari Road, Daryaganj
New Delhi 110 002

*Sales Centres:*

Allahabad Bengaluru Chandigarh
Chennai Hyderabad Jaipur Kathmandu
Kolkata Mumbai



Typeset in 11.5 pt. Aldine401 BT by
Mindways Design
1410 Chiranjiv Tower,
43 Nehru Place
New Delhi 110 019

Printed in India by
Rekha Printers Pvt. Ltd.
A-102/1 Okhla Industrial Area, Phase-II
New Delhi-110 020

*For those who have left us, but continue to stay, an ache,*
*a memory in our heart . . .*
*For those who cannot speak, but tell us so much . . .*
*For the wilds . . . with the hope that they flourish, forever.*

# Contents

# Introduction

One strong conviction that governed the idea of this book, and to some extent the choice of writings, is my belief in the power of words. My interest in wildlife is not born of a childhood spent in nature's lap. I had a very urban upbringing, and my association with wildlife was largely restricted to an occasional visit to Gir, the last refuge of the Asiatic lion. Those days, lions were usually baited with terrified buffalo calves, to lure the feline predator for VIP visitors. The other 'wild' encounters—if you can call them that—were visits to zoos and circuses. These excursions—erringly perceived as entertainment and educational pursuits—did little to inspire within me any awe for the natural world. Indeed, I found the concept distasteful, and these visits left, even at an early age, only a sense of shame and guilt. But that is another debate, and I digress. The point I am trying to make is that my passion for the wilds—and it is an emotive affair—has literary roots. I have devoured book after book on the subject, haunting libraries and pavement book-vendors (who had the money for new books?). The first 'animal' book that piqued my interest was James Herriot's delightful and thoroughly addictive account of a vet's life in the English countryside. Not nature writing, strictly speaking. Yet, Herriot had an art of bringing animals 'to life'. His intricate portrayal of his patients and their idiosyncrasies drew you in, and your involvement in his works was complete. Herriot was the first 'animal' writer I encountered, and he set the ball rolling. Next was Gerald Durrell, with his fascinating repertoire of books, including the absolutely hilarious *My Family and Other Animals*. There was no looking back after that—and the list of writers-naturalists who have shaped my thoughts and way of life is evolving. There were writers from foreign shores, like John Muir, Rachel Carson, Henry David Thoreau, and Peter Mathieson, whose compelling works were a major influence. The other powerful works came from biologists and conservationists like Jane Goodall, Dian Fossey and Ian Douglas-Hamilton, whose path-breaking studies have influenced generations. Each of them opened a window, planted a seed, but it was the treatise on our native flora and fauna that had me truly hooked. They were more real—they were closer home. The elephants, the lions, the tigers – they were in our backyard. In a sense, they were *ours*—to explore, to experience, and to protect.

I will not go too far back in history, but I must make a mention of the contribution made by the Mughal emperors, who comprehensively documented their observations on India's faunal wealth, notably the founder of the dynasty, Emperor Babar (*Babarnama*), and then Jehangir, who was the greatest naturalist of the Mughal empire. He was an astute observer, and his *Tuzk-e-Jehangiri* has detailed and animated descriptions of wildlife. He used several local artists, the most prominent being Ustad Mansur, to make life-like drawings of the occupants of his menagerie. The first drawing of the now-extinct Dodo is attributed to his court. India's legendary 'Birdman', Salim Ali, explores at length this little known side of the Mughals in *The Moghul Emperors of India as Naturalists and Sportsmen*.

Game hunters wrote most of our early natural history literature. 'Shikar' has left a mixed legacy in the subcontinent. There is no doubt that hunting played a major part in the decline of wild animals and birds. Yet, in the bygone era, there was no naturalist as ardent as the hunter in pursuit of his quarry. He was well-versed in jungle lore, was a keen observer, and kept meticulous records—the latter being especially true of the colonial hunter. Hunting stories may seem out of context today; nevertheless, in the annals of natural history they occupy an important and irreplaceable place. They are the chronicles of our vanishing natural heritage, the imprinted proof of a lost world.

The early colonial era marked a succession of naturalists, and this growing interest of sharing field-observations led to the formation of the Bombay Natural History Society (1883), whose journals are one vast treasure trove. 'EHA' or E.H. Aitkin, was one among the eight founder-members of the society, and easily the wittiest naturalist-author of his time. He was unusual—deviating from the prevalent big-game mania, focusing instead on the occupations of the crab and other such smaller creatures, with considerable finesse and aplomb. He wrote with compassion, entreating the hunter to 'cherish the tender place in your nature, which feels a pang when you pick up the little corpse, so happy two minutes ago.' He warned the collector to beware, 'lest you begin to feel that a rare bird is not so much a bird but a *specimen.*' EHA was one of a kind.

James Forsyth, a forester, is noted for his seminal *Highlands of Central India*, in which he mentions, almost in passing, 'I have several times come across and shot the hunting leopard.' That was in the mid-eighteenth century; a hundred years later, the hunting leopard or cheetah was extinct in India. G.P. Sanderson details the elaborate and cruel *kheddah* or trapping of wild elephants in Mysore for the royal stable. Shikar lore is almost synonymous with Jim Corbett, an exceptionally fine writer. The legendary hunter was also a pioneer conservationist, who worried about the fading fortunes of the tiger. But sometimes, I wonder: What is his best-remembered legacy? *The Man-eaters of Kumaon* continues to be a bestseller today. While Corbett took pains to stress that it was circumstances that made a tiger a man-eater, did his thrilling accounts leave a subconscious impression that all tigers and leopards are dangerous beasts?

Macho hunting accounts, such as those written by Kenneth Anderson, come with another rider—an obsession with big game; tigers, leopards, gaur, elephants, and wild buffaloes—few looked beyond the mega-fauna.

The debate whether hunting tales should form part of this collection plagued my mind. Not just because other—and very worthy—anthologies have done an admirable job of putting together excellent prose on hunting, but mainly because of a sense of discomfort with the idea. Hunting was, and is, an unequal sport – it's 'advantage man' all along. The idea of viewing free, wild creatures through the barrel of the gun is disagreeable, to say the least, even more so in current climes when yesterday's 'game' faces extinction today. In the age of ecological enlightenment, the yesteryear carnage seems best relegated to the past.

There were many other naturalist-writers. Salim Ali's autobiographical *Fall of the Sparrow* and E.P. Gee's *Wildlife of India*, are almost biblical in their value. Then came the more contemporary conservationists like David Attenborough, George Schaller, and closer home, Billy Arjan Singh (another former hunter who took to preservation passionately. Billy passed away as the new year dawned, on 1 January 2010, and we have lost the tiger's most fierce defender, the most dedicated soldier), and later, Valmik Thapar and Bittu Sahgal. Then, there are those who may not necessarily be conservationists but are sensitive, established wordsmiths who wrote classics that left an indelible impression on your heart and mind. Ruth Padel's *Tigers in Red Weather*, Amitav Ghosh's *The Hungry Tide* and Douglas Adam's *Last Chance to See,* are those that immediately come to mind.

I have omitted (with a heavy heart) the past masters, concentrating instead on current works, simply because that is too vast a treasury and demands a collection in itself. Admittedly, I have slipped, seduced by the powerful, evocative voice of M. Krishnan and F.W. Champion. You will understand; *of course* you will. I could not ignore M. Krishnan. For any wildlifer, Krishnan is simply a religion—no words can do justice to his phenomenal contribution to nature writing. F.W. Champion was amazing. In the day of the big game hunter, Champion pioneered wildlife photography, even as he worried whether 'the photographer interferes with sport and happiness of wild animals.' Extraordinary! There were so many authors whose absence leaves the book bereft: EHA, Salim Ali, Billy Arjan Singh . . . another book perhaps?

As much a pleasure rambling about (and reading) these books is, I think I have jumped the gun. Let me backtrack a bit and ask you to ponder a basic question: What does the term *wildlife* mean? In the dictionary it's simply 'flora and fauna'. Ill-defined, I think, or maybe way too precise to encompass its import. So, again, what *does* wildlife mean? What picture does it conjure? Of dense green forests teeming with great animals and birds, of tigers hunting, gigantic elephants, herds of deer—a constant blur of teeming mega-fauna? What does wildlife imply to the average man? Is it something to see, like a fort or a museum? Is it an adventure, a safari? Is it our stab at being 'primitive' even as we scurry from a jeep to a resort? Is it a medley of myths and prejudices born of portrayal in films and popular culture? Does it invoke fear? Perhaps, a vague stir in the conscience as one reads and hears about its continued carnage in the media? Or, does it simply not occupy our minds at all?

A scary thought, but not beyond the realm of possibility. Our lives are insular, dissociated with nature. Milk is sourced from tetra packs, and outdoors is where the car is. And animals? At best, they are our pet dog, cat or goldfish. A cynical view admittedly, but for the urban global citizen, it is largely true.

Even scarier—is it People *vs* Wildlife, Us *vs* Them? I won't go into the devastation we have wrought on the earth and our natural heritage; suffice to say for now that our hunger and greed and incessant consumption have all but destroyed wildlife and its habitats, till wilderness in the truest sense of the word has almost ceased to exist. I have watched (in horror) 'Item Bomb Talent Hunt'—a dance contest—on TV, in a tiny hamlet in one of the remotest valleys of Ladakh, dived off a lonely island only to spot an empty packet of 'Uncle Chips' among incredible coral reefs, and 'spotted' chewing-tobacco pouches littering pristine rainforests. Nothing is too far way, or too remote. Civilisation—such as it is—has conquered it all.

I will not attempt to explain what wildlife is. It is much beyond the composite of tigers and elephants and birds and beetles and toads—and the space they occupy. I will let the book 'talk'.

Words are voices (without the noise!), voices that you have chosen to listen to, if you have picked up the book, and taken a decision to read. This book is, to use the much-used adage, the 'voice of the voiceless', of vanishing landscapes, of a fading wilderness, of endangered wildlife. By virtue of being an anthology, it is a spectrum of messages, without (I hope) being a muddled cacophony. Admittedly, the voices are erratic, diverse, as they must be given the diversity and the sheer scale of the subject.

The choice of the pieces is eclectic, not adhering to any pattern, save for a hope that it leaves an imprint on your heart and touches a chord. And that each presents a different facet and mood, perhaps just give a glimpse of the sheer scale of the diversity. It also talks of the threats and the battles, because the luxury of just imbibing the joys of nature is not ours anymore. Any of us who enjoy wildlife is faced with its impending doom. None of us can afford not to care.

Take heart though—there is no message *per se*. An exception may be Kailash Sankhala's *Our Wild Heritage*, which focuses on the threats to our wildlife. Sankhala, the 'Tiger Man' of India, headed Project Tiger when it was born in 1973. I was tempted to include his commentary on the tiger, or his equally enlightening work on the Indian desert. But this chapter sold itself by its sheer tenacity—authored more than three decades back, we still grapple with the same problems highlighted in the piece, only they are more magnified.

The book is largely a celebration of our wilds—be it an exhilarating day at Ranthambhore with India's best known tiger-expert, Valmik Thapar, or the 'lowly' caterpillar in an engrossing tale of fiction on a subject most wildlifers—obsessed as we are with mega-fauna—would pay least attention to.

The other thought I have tried to convey, through the delightful piece by Janaki Lenin, is that wildlife is not 'out there'. Janaki, with her wonderful sense of humour, chronicles and rambles about 'her husband and other animals' with whom she shares her home. She is fortunate, of course, that her house is on the outskirts of a metro, but if you have the eyes and the ears (and with a little bit of effort) you will have many a pleasurable moment with the wildlife in your backyard. I stay in the heart of a city, but a water bowl and birdseed have totted up my garden bird list to nearly thirty. *Memories of Birding in India* is the other story which opens a window to the avian life in the city.

India is the land of the tiger, and this charismatic ambassador of our wilds ensures that here too, he dominates the literary landscape, as the book meanders through the mystic mangroves of Sundarbans, and then onto the Mecca of tiger worshippers – Corbett National Park.

Ullas Karanth injects the voice of reason—rationalising a conservation module with science as its base. As he explains, 'Mere passion for the cause is not enough: conservationists need to act in reasonable ways to make their passion work for tigers on ground. We have to act, but based on careful reasoning.'

India's other rare big cat, the Asiatic lion, too finds a scientific voice in A.J.T. Johnsingh. I have a soft spot for the leopard—beautiful, agile, solitary, smart, strong, and a survivor battling the many odds stacked against it. I have followed the leopard's increasingly precarious fate closely, and I found no story as telling, as beautifully touching as Ruskin Bond's work of fiction.

*A Letter to Teddy* continues in similar vein. Fiction? Conventionally speaking, maybe. But there is nothing as terrifyingly real as the cruel fate of the dancing bears, evocatively told in the voice of 'Mama Bear', culled from the relatively unknown, but powerful book, *Voices in My Head*.

The elephant is Ganesha, the God of good fortune. Yet, it is killed for its ivory, and in the repeated cross-fire of man–elephant conflict. *Gabbar Singh and Chomsky* does not dwell on either; it is an entertaining account of the ways of the pachyderm, or rather one stubborn, wilful and endearing pachyderm. *The Mating Tusker* is the one that draws attention on the issue of the elephant's dwindling habitat, and its disastrous consequences.

*Winds of Change* weaves many tales, at the heart of which is a vanishing landscape—the loss of wilderness, of ancient rhythms and a way of life as development makes inroads into our remotest regions.

The *Homo sapien* is land-obsessed; even when we think wildlife the picture we draw is of lush rainforests. Rarely does our imagination stray to the fecund forests of the sea—coral reefs, sea grasses, and the incredible marine diversity. *Looking for Mermaids* is the author's quest to highlight the plight of the dugong, a very rare sea mammal, while Shekar Dattatri takes us to a remote beach in Orissa to witness the *arribada*, the spectacular natural phenomenon of lakhs of turtles nesting on their natal beach.

There are few feel-good stories in conservation. Good news is rare; all wild creatures and habitats come with their baggage of threats and problems. And it just gets worse as human population and greed explodes, as development eats into habitats, as our world grows warmer by the minute. In this grim scenario, the Munzala story—the discovery of a new species of macaque—is a rare exception. I will leave you with that hope—that despite our destructive ways, there is new life on this planet, that the forest still holds its magic and mysteries. . . .

# Five Encounters

*M. Krishnan*

*M. Krishnan was an inspiration, if not a religion, to generations of naturalists. Krishnan worked his way through many jobs, the most enduring of which was employment with the Maharajah of Sandur. The job was dreary, but there were compensations—it afforded him the opportunity to travel, thus allowing him to nurture his love for nature. In 1949, when the state was merged into the Union of India, Krishnan returned to Madras and for the rest of his life made a living—if precarious—from writing and photography. From 1950 onwards, he penned a fortnightly column for* The Statesman, *called 'The Country Notebook', which continued till the day he died. Krishnan was an oddity; as Ramchandra Guha, who edited a collection of his works so succinctly puts it, 'He was exceptional in his generation for being a conservationist qua conservationist, not part of the repentant butchers club.' Unlike most of his contemporaries, he focused not only on megafauna but wrote with similar measure of affection of the owlet or the toad, as he would the tiger or the elephant. He won a Padma Shri as well as a place in the Global 500 Roll of Honour of the United Nations Environment Programme. He served the Indian Board for Wildlife for three decades. And though he had varied 'un-natural' interests—from cricket to Carnatic music—it is as a true ecological patriot that he is fondly remembered, and missed.*

For over six decades, right from my college days, I have been wandering over the forests and scrublands of India, investigating their wildlife. And in all that time, and in spite of dangerous risks run in ignorance of animal ways, only on four occasions have I been in the shadow of imminent death – once when I almost walked into an enormous sloth bear while looking up at the fruits on a tree, and thrice when following wild elephants on foot by myself—it is best to go alone, for a companion doubles the chances of being detected. There was no time to feel frightened then: one is wholly preoccupied with escape, and it is only after escaping that one's liver turns to water and the belated fright-reaction sets in. Strangely, it is not these crises that I remember most vividly, but comparatively minor encounters with wild animals that excited me and filled me with wonder. I recount some here.

~

Long ago, I was in service in a small Princely State in the Deccan, in a narrow, green valley girt round with a double ring of hills. The flora was distinctive (as noted nearly a century ago by J.S. Gamble in his monumental *Flora of the Presidency of Madras*), the bird life was rich, and the mammalian fauna varied, featuring sambar, wild pigs and leopards, among the larger animals. My official duties were heavy and laborious, but compensated by unspoilt nature all around.

I do not shoot, and disapprove of all hunting, but my best opportunities for seeing animals lay in joining the occasional shikar parties organised, usually just outside the state. If there was to be a beat, I liked to stay with the beaters; that way one could see many birds and small animals usually missed: hares, mongooses, monitors, snakes and the like. A hillside was being beaten towards the guns on top by a dozen men, and I had been posted as a stop—that is, to turn what came along a game patch back into the beat. It was almost evening, and I was standing where the path ran through a line of tall bushes, blocking the gap. In those days, I used to supplement my olive-green clothes with a cap having a deep peak and side-flaps to prevent incident light causing my spectacles to glint. I stood some distance from a bend in the path, and nothing came towards me. Then, as the beat was nearing its end, a pair of four-horned antelopes came tripping round the bend.

The *chowsingha*, or four-horned antelope, is the only wild animal which, in the buck, has an additional pair of little knob-horns above the eyes and below the regular spike-horns on top of the head; the doe is hornless. Even otherwise it is unique—exclusively Indian, without any close relative anywhere, capriciously distributed across the country on low hilltops, given to drinking every day during the hottest hours, and unlike most antelopes, not gregarious but going about by itself or in a pair. It is small and compactly built, just two-foot high, a greyish brown on top and furry white below, and has a dainty gait.

I stood stock-still and the pair came tripping along in no hurry, almost side-by-side. They did not see me till they were quite near, only some ten feet away, and then froze instantly, and half-squatted. Then, they rose in a brace in the air and flew right overhead, to my incredulous surprise. The most athletic of our animals, the leopard, could not have jumped so high from a standing start—in my thick-soled boots and cap I stood six-foot tall, and they cleared my head with a cubit to spare! By the time I could turn around, they had disappeared into the bush cover behind me, and I just stood there, almost unable to believe my eyes. Then, slowly my amazement turned to a feeling of relief and gladness, that they had escaped the beat so comprehensively.

~

The road from Masinagudi to the Moyar Hydel Project is over a dozen km long. On one side of it is the concrete-flanked Maravakandi canal, carrying the waters of the project, and on the other, the north-eastern border of the Mudumalai sanctuary. This part of the preserve features alternating stretches of dense forests and clearings, and wild elephants frequent it after the rains. The rainwater collects in shallow, linear pools in some of the clearings, and elephants like to drink from them, standing five or six in a row. I had long wanted to photograph them drinking here, and that forenoon offered the opportunity.

A herd was approaching a clearing through the forest, a large and boisterous herd to judge by its many voices. Old Mara and I stood on the road, facing the clearing. He knew the area well, and I did not, and he said the herd would cross the clearing, enter the belt of forest beyond, and proceed through it to a sandy clearing still further of where there was a chain of pools: we should give them time to get to the water, and then take the path they had taken through the trees, the only path there was to those pools. I do not like having anyone with me on such occasions, but needed Mara's guidance, for it is easy to lose one's way in dense cover.

We did not have to wait long. The elephants came onto the clearing in small groups, twenty of them, and entered the belt of trees beyond. We waited ten minutes for any lagging behind to come out, and none came. We had to go quite some distance into the clearing to reach the point of entry into the tree cover, and overshot it. And as we were retracing our steps, we saw that two cow elephants had entered the clearing just behind us, and were crossing it towards the trees. They were to our left, between us and the road.

There was no bush to hide us, to try running away would most probably provoke a charge, and standing still we were conspicuous. We sank to the ground and crouched low. 'Take off your clothes,' whispered Mara urgently. For a moment I did not understand him, then did. He had already stripped, and gathering the fresh elephant dung in front of him in his hands, was smearing it all over himself. Quickly getting out of my clothes, I followed suit. It was nauseating, but necessary. The ground breeze was blowing directly from us towards the elephants—the over-powering stench of the still-warm dung would mask our man-smell.

The two cows sauntered to the trees ahead of them and went in. To our consternation, we noticed that a cow with a young calf, and behind them a big tusker, had now come onto the clearing from behind us. We continued to crouch and stay still. Slowly, the cow and the calf crossed to the trees in front, but the tusker stopped directly in a line with us, and very near; he was less than the length of a cricket pitch, to my left. I dared not turn to look, but after what seemed an unbearable ten minutes, and was probably too, I glanced sideways. He was standing at ease, flapping his ears (always a sign of contentment), with his trunk lowered right to the ground—and he had sharp, curved, murderous-looking tusks! After an age, I stole another sideway look, and he was still there, flapping his ears.

The most remarkable thing in existence is not the behaviour of wild elephants but of the human mind. By now my curiosity had overcome my dreadful apprehensions, and inch by inch I turned a little to my left, to watch. The tusker was standing on a patch of *Mimosa pudica* (the sensitive plant, the ground herb whose tiny, feathery leaves shrink and close when touched) covering the ground in a flat, dark-green spread. The spread was in bloom, with a great many tiny flower-heads, like minute, pink badminton balls, dotting it all over. Laboriously, the great beast was gathering the flowers in the crook of his trunk-tip and conveying them carefully to his mouth!

After a while, he too crossed over and disappeared into the tree cover, and getting to our feet, we raced to the road, crossed it, and plunged into the Maravakandi canal. The water here is never clean and clear, but there was a distinct current, and in no time at all it had washed our skin free of every trace of elephant dung. In my hurry, I had left my clothes behind in the clearing and sent Mara to get them, while I climbed out and let the sun and air dry me.

(*P.S.:* I can find no reference to elephants fancying *Mimosa pudica* flowers in the literature on the animal, but can vouch for this authoritatively. Incidentally, the flowers have a faintly acidic taste in the human mouth.)

~

I have seldom photographed animals from a hide. I have often used treetop hides overlooking a forest pool or path to observe wild elephants in safety, unknown to them, but taken very few pictures of them then. And at the Guindy National Park around the Madras Raj Bhavan, I felt the need for a ground-hide to study the native blackbuck and the introduced *chital* closer than I could otherwise.

I need not explain why I felt this need, except to say it was for evidence to substantiate my reasons for chital thriving in places into which they had been newly introduced, to the detriment of the native herbivores. Preliminary reconnaissance disclosed a further problem. It was no use setting up a ground-hide at a selected spot. At Guindy, men are constantly moving about, and the animals, while used to human proximity, keep their distance and shift ground frequently. I needed a portable hide.

It then occurred to me that with a modification of what I wore on the field, no hide was necessary. Over the years, I have acquired the ability to stay still and to move, if I must, in slow-motion. My stained and patched brownish-green trousers and bush-shirt were inconspicuous, and if I had a light, wide-brimmed hat from which a veil could be hung, to mask my face, that should do. A khaki soft hat, such as some policemen wear, seemed best, and I bought one at a second-hand clothes' shop. Then I consulted an acquaintance, who had worked as a seamstress, for the veil, and she advised not a fixed veil, but a number of slip-knot nooses around the brim from which thin green twigs could be hung, for better camouflage and to enable me to see through readily. This she was kind enough to stitch on herself, and armed with my new headgear, I set out for Guindy after lunch.

By three o'clock I found a promising spot, with no men nearby, and a flat stone at the foot of a wood-apple tree to sit on. The ground in front was bare and brown with spare patches of low herbage, but there were some tall bushes. A soft-haired, leafy twiner with a sticky white juice festooned two of the bushes: it was in fruit, hung with long, green, paired follicles along its pliant coils—obviously, a plant of the Aclepiadaceae (*Pergularia daemia*, as identified later). Taking the hat out of my handbag, I collected lengths of the twiner complete with follicles, so that the twin fruits would stabilise the pendent veil of their lengths. Securing them in place, I put on the hat and ensconced myself on the stone slab.

Soon, it was apparent that I had overdone things a bit. The hanging greenery in front of my face was too closely spaced and in the way of clear vision, even of easy breathing, and the twiner had a strong, foul smell. Thanks to the slipknots, this could be easily remedied, but as I raised my hand to do so, five chital came into view, feeding steadily, towards me—three adult hinds, a young stag in velvet, and a half-grown fawn. I froze, and watched.

They were grazing and browsing, cropping such ground vegetation as there was, and feeding on the foliage of some bushes: they were partial to the follicles I had left behind on top of the bushes, standing up on their hind legs to get at them. By now they were very close, and I wondered when they would spot me. Then, the hind in the lead trotted right up and snipped a follicle off my hat, and at once the rest joined in, tugging at the fruits from all around so that the hat stayed miraculously wobbling on my head. Then it fell away, and at once they scattered and bolted.

Chital are short-scented. How was it, then, that from so near they had failed to notice my sweaty man-smell? Had the stronger smell of the fresh-cut twiner masked it? I do not know the answer to these questions. I never tried the experiment again.

~

I made an early start on elephant-back, so as to be at the expanse of up-and-coming grass in time to see what was feeding there, but on the way, we chanced on a huge lone bull gaur and followed him for almost two hours. It was nearing noon when we reached the slope lush with fresh-grown tall grass. There was no animal to be seen, but something had fed there quite recently. There was a darkish furrow in places going up the sea of bright green grass tips. It was Maasthi, my mahout and companion, who noticed this first and pointed it out to me.

We went a little way up, for a closer look. It had rained in the night, and the ground was moist and impressionable. The unmistakable, so-human footprints of a large sloth bear zigzagged up the rise, and alongside the back the grass had been bitten off in sheaves. I remarked to Maasthi that the bear must have had quite a feast here. He shook his head.

'Bears do not eat grass,' he said.

I assured him they did, and that I had seen them feeding on fresh grass with gusto. Maasthi had great faith in my knowledge of animals, and had often consulted me when in doubt; he had also told me things I did not know, which I subsequently found to be factual. He knew perfectly well that I would not make a positive assertion unless it was true, but this once he was unable to accept my authority. He said that I must have seen what I had seen elsewhere, not here—here, bears did not eat grass.

I asked what animal, then, had guzzled the tall grass here so zestfully—there were no other tracks on the ground, not a single hoof-print. However, I did not argue the point further. I was already feeling puckish, and it would take us an hour and a half to get back to the rest house and lunch. We decided to be at this pasture early next day.

And when we were there next morning, the bear was also there, busy with his breakfast. For a while, we watched from behind a thick-boled tree. He was facing away from us, but we could see him quite clearly. He fed choosily, taking his time, selecting a tussock of tender grass and bending its top to his mouth with a paw, to munch it up. I was keen on a photograph if I could get one, but had to get closer—he was already halfway up the rise. Not following in his wake, but keeping to one side of it, we moved the elephant up, and at once he began to hurry. He had his back to us still, but had somehow sensed our presence. I called a halt so as not to panic him, and he went right up to the bare, stony top of the rise and stopped. He still faced away from us, and did not turn round to look, but bending his head low down so that the crown almost touched the ground, looked at us from between his legs! For nearly a minute he stared at us like this, and then went down the other side of the rise at a bobbing run to vanish into the forest.

Maasthi turned to me in utter puzzlement. 'Would we have seemed upside down to the bear?' he asked.

~

Late in the year, when cyclones hit the south-eastern coast, I was at Point Calimere in a tiny cottage on the beach. Very late one afternoon, it suddenly grew dark, black rain clouds blotted out the sun, and a high wind sprang up. By the time I could close and bolt the door and the two small windows, the storm was upon me.

Torrential rain beat down on the steep tiles, thunderclaps crashed overhead and the wind's voice rose to a banshee shriek. Not a drop of water penetrated my retreat, built to withstand the elements. My food was being brought from outside, and I could not hope for dinner, but I thought this primeval fury could not last all night, and sat down stoically to wait. There was no let-up, and by four in the morning I fell asleep to the strident lullaby of the cyclone.

A hammering on my door awoke me, and when I opened it, it was bright outside and seven o'clock already. The forester was there with a flask of hot coffee and a substantial pack-breakfast. I was feeling famished, but ate sparingly, for it was important to go out at once to see what damage the vegetation and animal life had suffered. The forester vetoed the outing: there was an almost overpowering wind blowing just above the ground, and he had experienced considerable difficulty getting to me. He was lath-thin and insubstantial. I was almost twice his weight and in hard condition. Picking up a light 35 mm camera, I ploughed my way to the sea.

I have never known anything like that two-level groundwind. Up to knee height there was no stir of air, and then till well above one's head there was an almost solid blast of faintly sibilant wind, repulsing one. I had to lean into it to force my way through. The sea, flat and placid at Point Calimere, was calm again, but it had run amok in the night. The wreck lay scattered high up the shore, shellfish, squishy mollusks, broken-up crustaceans, bits and pieces of long-drowned wood, and small fishes. Nothing large, and surprisingly, no seaweed.

I was astonished at the way the vegetation had survived the cyclone's violence. Trees and bushes here are tough and flat-topped: they had bowed their crowns to the raging wind, and except for twigs and branchlets torn off and flung around, had escaped unscathed. The ground vegetation was unaffected: in places, ephemeral little pools had drowned it, but the sand would suck in the water by nightfall.

Rounding a bend, I came upon a pair of jackals scavenging on what the sea had thrown up, and seeing me they decamped into the bushes. A little beyond, some two hundred brown-headed gulls were sitting tight on the wet sand in a long row, all facing the air current, waiting for the wind to die down. They ignored me as I passed very close by them and took some pictures. Further still, I came to what had been a little bay the previous day, now scooped by the storm into a miniature lagoon extending far up the shore and about seventy yards across. The opposite bank was topped by ground vegetation and through its tangle I could just glimpse what looked like the heads of some large sea-birds.

The sea at Point Calimere is quite shallow for quite some distance from the shore. A few days earlier, I had spent an hour standing waist-deep in the sea, photographing the assorted crowd of gulls flying around the incoming boats for the guts of the catch being tossed out. I had been sternly warned by the fishermen not to be so foolish; there might be sting-rays in the shallows that could inflict a fearful injury.

Far out to sea, I could see dolphins circling and occasionally leaping up into the air. I had seen them here in the sea many times, always too far away to be clearly watched. There was nothing else in sight, and I wanted to have a look at the birds on the further bank before turning back.

To go all the way round would be to progress through the buffeting wind, but I could easily wade across. I walked into the water, which came only up to my knees, and then to my waist; and I was half-way through when I was suddenly almost shoulder-deep in it. Evidently, the storm-tossed sea had dug into the sandy bottom here, and it was best to get out of the trough. Holding my camera at head height, I turned round. Something long and live and heavy brushed gently against me in the water, and I stopped dead. Again, something long and thick brushed my back, hardly touching me. Then, the dolphins were swirling around me, in a whirligig of *joie de vivre*.

There were half-a-dozen of them, circling at high speed and skimming the surface now and again to throw up an impetuous spray. I just stood there, holding the camera pressed to my head, utterly spellbound. These were common dolphins, eight-foot long and sleekly streamlined, steel-grey on top and white below with a yellowish streak along the flanks, and the jaws in a beak armed with teeth that could probably bite through one's arm. I felt no fear, only amazement and wonder. Then, as suddenly as they had come, they raced away, far into the sea. I have seldom felt so thrilled.

Dolphins are the only wild animals that have a strange affinity to humanity. Right from Greek mythology to Mediterranean tales there are accounts of their friendliness towards men. I had read these accounts, and thought them only charming legends.

Excerpted from *Nature's Spokesman: M. Krishnan and Indian Wildlife*, Edited by Ramachandra Guha, Penguin Books, India

# Curiosity in Animals

F.W. CHAMPION

*At a time when most naturalists and authors viewed wildlife through the barrel of the gun, F.W. Champion was the exception. His 'weapon' was the camera, and even that made Champion ponder whether photography would 'interfere with the happiness of wild creatures.' He worried whether 'the cage could anyway compare in the tiger's mind with the vast spaces of his native jungle.' He hated giving shooting permits as his job in the Imperial Forestry Service demanded, and is known to have done so in areas where he knew there were no tigers. Champion's quarry was the perfect photograph; indeed, he was one of the pioneers of camera trapping, whereby the animal would trigger the camera and flash, taking pictures of itself. A modernised version of this system is still used to count, and save tigers! He was a rare early conservationist who detailed his experiences in* With a Camera in Tigerland *and* The Jungle in Sunlight and Shadow.

*An acute observer of wildlife, and a passionate protector, he hoped that his writings and photographs would encourage sympathy for wild creatures. The following piece is especially intriguing, and has Champion ruminating (or rather making a case for) about the presence of curiosity in animals.*

I suppose we all agree with Byron that curiosity really is a vice, although it is not one that would rank very high (or perhaps, I should say low) among the numerous sins of this world; at least I hope not, for I must confess to a marked curiosity concerning the home lives of the wild creatures that are fellow-inhabitants of the jungle with me. Also, I sincerely hope that the objects of my curiosity do not resent my friendly probing into their private affairs, or make them look upon me as an impertinent press-photographer who spends his time taking pictures that they would much prefer not to be taken. Anyhow, I always feel that some of my photographs, however shy my subjects may be of having them made, may perhaps help to encourage that growing sympathy for wild creatures, which is so marked a feature of this post-War period, and that in itself is sufficient justification for my having made them, with or without permission.

However, even if curiosity be considered as a vice among ourselves, it is not necessarily so in the case of other animals. Quite apart from the five primary senses which wild animals possess, sometimes in a greater and sometimes in a lesser degree than ourselves, the creatures of the jungle have many special traits of their own, often more or less as a general characteristic of the species, but quite frequently peculiar to the particular individual. One of the most interesting of these traits is that of curiosity, which certainly appears to exist to a considerable degree in some animals, although the motives underlying curiosity will generally be found to be more primitive than in the case of human beings.

The vast majority of the actions of wild animals are governed by three dominant motives: the necessity of obtaining sufficient food and water, for wild animals all have to fend for themselves and cannot, like ourselves, rely upon servants or money to supply their needs; the instinct of self-preservation, which is just as important to wild creatures as to mankind; and the urge to propagate the species, which is Nature's way of ensuring the continuation of the race. Nevertheless, curiosity certainly does sometimes cause wild animals to do things which normally they would not do, and indeed at times induces them to run unnecessary risks. This is particularly the case with young animals, as with children, and is really one of Nature's ways of teaching them what is safe and what is unsafe; of helping them to learn quickly what is good to eat and what should be avoided; of educating them up to the standard which is required if they are to enjoy a happy and successful life.

The female sex in animals—as in human beings!—seems to be more curious than the male, and sambar hinds perhaps suffer more from an excessively developed strain of curiosity than any other creatures in the jungle. Quite frequently, they will stand and stare, with widely dilated eyes, at a tame elephant or a motorcar, and if no sudden movement be made, they will sometimes come right up to the object which has excited their interest and examine it carefully. I can recall many cases of sambar hinds when their insatiable curiosity managed to overcome their natural instinct of distrust, which, in the interests of self-preservation, must always compete with the urge to examine strange things. I well remember one case in particular. I was wandering about the jungles on a tame elephant, looking for photographic subjects when suddenly I came upon a sambar hind standing on the edge of a bamboo clump. Wild elephants were quite common in the neighbourhood, so that she was obviously more or less familiar with the appearance of these huge creatures. Her large sensitive ears immediately shot forward, her eyes began to dilate, and one could almost hear her saying to herself, 'Well, here is one of those great elephants quite close to me. How I would love to stop and have a good look, but is it quite safe?' Realising what was passing in the sambar's mind, I immediately made my elephant 'freeze', and decided to wait, as motionless as possible, so that I might see what the hind would do. For a few moments she hesitated, curiosity and timidity competing with each other, and the slightest movement on my part would have resulted in her precipitate departure. My tame elephant stood like a rock, however, as though she understood what I wanted, and at last the hind, deciding that there was little to fear, began gingerly to approach. Every now and then the elephant, worried by flies, would flap one of her great ears, and the first time this happened the hind was so startled that she jumped about a foot in the air. The second time the jump was less, and soon she became accustomed to the movements of the elephant's ears. By this time she was only some six or seven yards away and following her appeared a second and then a third hind, all of which seemed fascinated by the sight of the great beast in front of them. Their fascination and curiosity gradually drew them nearer and nearer until finally all three were within a very few yards of the motionless elephant, by which time they decided that there was nothing more to see. They, therefore, began to make a meal of the luscious grass in which they were standing, every now and then lifting up their heads to have yet another look at the elephant standing silently in front of them. This went on for about half an hour until finally they moved on, and I was able to release the elephant—which had behaved magnificently—from the strain of standing to attention for such a long time. There is no doubt whatever, but that the behaviour of these three sambar hinds was due to pure curiosity, and most shikaris could probably remember somewhat similar examples that they have come across during their wanderings in the great jungles of India.

Monkeys are also extremely curious animals. A large mirror placed at a convenient spot where monkeys abound, will often produce most amusing behaviour on the part of these creatures, which in many ways bear such a close resemblance to ourselves. They will come and look into the mirror and then go round to the back in search of the reflection which they see in it but cannot touch or find. Backwards and forwards they will go, making faces and clawing at the mirror, and all with no result. I once had an uncanny experience with a mirror and a domestic cat that had run wild and taken to looting food from forest rest-houses. I was sitting one evening in the central room of such a rest-house, when I was startled to hear an appalling noise coming from the bedroom. Creeping to the door I peeped in and there was the cat sitting on the dressing-table, spitting fire and clawing at its own reflection in the mirror. The whole episode was absolutely comical, as mixed with the look of rage on the cat's face was one of bewilderment at not being able to claw the supposed rival, which always struck out at the same moment!

Tigers can be extremely inquisitive at times. On one occasion, I wished to erect an automatic flashlight trap over a path passing through the domain of a particularly fine tiger, which we knew for years as 'The King of Chaukham', but which we never succeeded in photographing. As this fine animal was notoriously cunning, I fixed the cameras and flashlight in position early one afternoon, so as to avoid making a noise in the evening for fear I should disturb my quarry. While arranging the cameras I heard a sambar call once or twice quite close by, and I formed a suspicion that the tiger was somewhere near, and was possibly watching what I was doing, but I was not quite certain. However, on returning just at dusk to join up the electric connections, I found that my suspicions had been justified, for there were the tracks of the tiger all round my cameras. He had obviously watched me arranging the photographic apparatus, and as soon as I was well out of the way, his curiosity caused him to come up in the middle of the afternoon—an unusual time for tigers to move about—and make a thorough examination of what I had been doing. He did not damage the cameras in any way, but needless to say, he did not fall into the photographic trap on that, or indeed any other night except once, and on the particular occasion the electric circuit unfortunately failed to work.

Another incident showing how inquisitive tigers can be, recently occurred in the foothill forests of the United Provinces. Their story as related to me was as follows:

> A certain sportsman drove his car out into the jungle one afternoon with the intention of setting up in a machan over a tiger-kill. When he had reached within a reasonable distance of his machan, he left his car on the road-side in charge of an orderly, and went off to the kill. The tiger did not put in an appearance, and on returning to his car he was astonished to find that the orderly left in charge had apparently disappeared. He called loudly but received no reply, until he thought of looking inside the car, where, to his amazement, he found the still terrified orderly crouching down beneath the dash-board. On questioning the man, it transpired that he was sitting quietly inside the car, when to his horror he saw a tiger walking towards him. He had no weapon of any sort, so he crouched down inside the car, hoping that the tiger would pass on. But his hopes were not fulfilled. The tiger paused, gazing at the weird object which obstructed his road, and then decided to come nearer to investigate. First, he walked round and sniffed at the various parts of the strange vehicle, apparently quite unaware of the presence of the quaking orderly inside. Then, he put his fore-paws on the bonnet, and looking

> in at the wind-screen, saw his own reflection in the glass. This gave him a shock, and he started to growl and paw at the reflection, quite unable to understand why his growls elicited no response, while the orderly, luckily for himself, remained hidden inside, comatose with fright. Finally, the tiger gave a snort of disgust, and departed, much to the relief of the most unwilling but undetected spectator. This was the story, as told by the orderly on his master's return, and from the clear pad-marks on the sandy road round the car and on the dusty bonnet, it could not have been very far from the truth.

It is interesting to recall that excellent old-time writer, 'Hawk-eye', once put forward the theory that one of the methods of hunting employed by tigers was to play upon the natural curiosity of the deer which form their chief prey. The suggestion was that the tiger would lie absolutely motionless and half-concealed in some open place, in such a way that a portion of his strikingly coloured skin would catch the eye of the deer. They would watch it for some time, and then finding that it did not move, they would gradually approach nearer and nearer to investigate, until finally the tiger, being now within striking distance, would hurl himself upon the hapless deer which he had thus lured to their destruction. The idea is attractive and just within the bounds of possibility, but unfortunately deers possess a strong sense of smell, so that the tiger would have to apply a good deal of deodorant if he wished to remove his own strong natural effluvium, which, accumulating owing to his remaining for some time in one spot, would it seems give him away almost every time. Even so, experienced human fowlers and trappers certainly do manage to catch animals and birds by taking advantage of the trait of curiosity displayed by some creatures, and many is the blackbuck that has met his end in this way, so there is no reason why the tiger also should not occasionally achieve success.

Hawk-eye's suggestion of tigers catching deer by playing on their curiosity receives considerable confirmation in the following story related to Mr W. Horst of the Indian Service of Engineers by a Nepalese Tharu named Ramji. This story refers to leopards catching monkeys, and I will give it in the man's own words, translated into English:

> Yes, Sahib, panthers are very bold and very cunning. Have you ever seen one catch a monkey? No. Well, I will tell you what four or five men from my village and I saw in the patch of jungle you beat through yesterday. We had been ploughing since dawn and sat down to rest under the big mango tree. There were some brown monkeys feeding quietly in the trees nearby, and suddenly one of them gave the usual sharp alarm call. We then heard the grunt of a charging panther, and saw a big one rush half-way up one of the smaller trees and then down again as the monkeys left it for the safety of the large jamun. He then charged over to the foot of the jamun and scratched up the grass and leaves round its roots. The excitement among the monkeys was now tremendous and they leapt about the branches in an agitated way, which was just what the panther expected and wanted. Had a monkey missed his hold or had a branch broken under one of them, the panther would have had his meal. But his luck was out and in a short time we saw him stretch himself out on the ground a few feet away from the tree and apparently go to sleep. The monkeys soon quieted down and we could see them looking down at the panther with the greatest interest. After a little while, one of the bigger ones climbed right over him and began to drop leaves and twigs on to him; but still there was no sign of movement. The other monkeys then began collecting closer and closer above him, and it was obvious that they couldn't understand what had

happened. One then climbed down a tree a short distance away and took a few steps towards the panther, but his nerve failed him and he dashed back to safety. There was still no movement from the panther, however, and soon three or four monkeys were on the ground, taking good care to keep well out of reach of claws and teeth. This continued for nearly half an hour, the monkeys drawing nearer and nearer, until at last one, bolder than the rest, actually touched the panther with his hand. This was what the patient hunter had been waiting for; he struck immediately and, seizing the inquisitive monkey, quietly carried his victim away to the patch of thick thorn out of which the pig broke yesterday. That, Sahib, shows the cunningness and the patience of a panther when he is hungry, and how the inquisitiveness of monkeys can lead them to their destruction.

Although I have never myself had the good fortune to see such a trick carried out, the story, to my mind, rings absolutely true. The Tharus are an illiterate simple race of jungle people, naturally truthful and straight-dealing, and there would be no object in romancing in this way. If leopards can catch monkeys by such a trick, it is more than possible that tigers can also be equally successful.

Among other animals of the jungle that exhibit curiosity is the wild elephant, which will often come within a few feet of a tame elephant brought up near him or her. This is partly due to the wild elephant's not being able to understand the curious mixture of scents emanating from a tame elephant on which men are riding. The scent of elephant attracts wild elephants, and the scent of man repels them. It is a very interesting, even if a somewhat nerve-racking amusement, to watch a wild elephant coming nearer and nearer, pausing every now and then to test the unusual mixture of scents and gazing with curious eyes at their cause. Wild elephants are also very quick to notice anything unusual placed in their chosen haunts, for which reason fences and boundary pillars have a very bad time. Curiosity causes them to examine such man-made erections, and resentment at what they possibly consider to be objectionable additions to their domain results in their being speedily destroyed.

I have read that in Africa, zebras and other animals will often race along parallel with motorcars as though curious to see if they can outpace them, and when they have succeeded in doing so, they will suddenly cross in front of the car. I have never noticed this habit among Indian animals, largely because most of them live in forests where there are too many trees to permit them to attempt to keep pace with a motorcar. Cattle, however, often run after cars or after tame elephants.

I have sometimes attempted to classify Indian jungle animals according to the amount of curiosity they display, but individuals vary so much that it is a very difficult task. I would certainly place sambar hinds first, closely followed by *Macacus* monkeys and peafowl, with elephants and tigers not far behind. Animals in which I have so far not noticed this trait as being particularly marked are leopards and sloth-bears, but this is more than likely due to lack of sufficient observation on my part. Indeed, some authors give bears, which are distinctly intelligent animals, a name for inquisitiveness, both in the wild and in captivity. It would appear that omnivorous animals would tend to be particularly inquisitive, as almost everything is worth examination in the hope that it may prove to be good to eat.

It is more than probable that if only we were sufficiently acquainted with their private lives, we should find that practically all the higher animals are inquisitive to a greater or lesser degree.

Excerpted from *The Jungle in Sunlight and Shadow*,
by F.W. Champion, 1934

# Memories of Birding in India

*PETER JACKSON*

*Peter Jackson was Reuters' chief correspondent in India in the 1950s and 1960s. He is a passionate naturalist, with a special interest in birds and the big cats. In this article he shares his memories of birding trips in India, and tells us of his first acquaintance with birds when trekking the Mount Everest in 1953 to report the successful Hillary–Tenzing expedition. It was the sight of the majestic Himalayan black eagle and 'groups of colourful birds' that he identified, with the help of Dr Salím Ali's book, as scarlet minivets, that piqued his interest. Incidentally, the legendry 'Birdman' of India was to later become a friend and companion on many a birding trip. During the sixteen years Jackson was based in Delhi, he spent most mornings roaming the countryside to see and photograph birds. Sunday was reserved for longer trips, especially to the Sultanpur Lake, which he helped protect as a sanctuary, with the aid of the then-Prime Minister, Mrs Indira Gandhi. He left India in 1970, switching from journalism to conservation, and went on to become the chairman of the IUCN (International Union for Conservation of Nature) Cat Specialist Group.*

I first visited India in 1945 when I was in the Royal Navy. I saw only the Bombay and Karachi ports and shopping areas. I can't remember birds, but the sight of whales leaping around our ship, off the Malabar coast, is etched in my memory.

When I returned in the early 1950s as a Reuters' correspondent, things were not as they were to be. New Delhi ended at Safdarjung, and a rough country road went out to the Qutub Minar. There were leopards in Tughlakabad; I never saw one, but was assured they were there. Friends went on a successful tiger hunt about thirty miles south of Delhi. Blackbuck and gazelles were sometimes seen. Few people other than locals were to be seen in the countryside; only occasionally did I see a few people at Suraj Kund.

On the east bank of the Yamuna, there were fields where I found coursers. Flamingos sometimes fed in the Yamuna, opposite the Red Fort, while the sandbanks, later planted with watermelon, were the nesting place for terns and the great stone plover.

A *jheel* at Najafgarh was a favourite haunt of waterbirds. It was a shallow basin that received excess monsoon water from the Yamuna through a drain, thereby reducing flooding further down the Yamuna. Later, lack of maintenance blocked the drain so that water remained in the jheel most of the year.

When the famous evolutionary biologist, Sir Julian Huxley, visited Delhi I took him to Najafgarh. The jheel being large, it was usual for the birds to be quite distant, but on this occasion the birds must have known my distinguished guest was present, for they put on a spectacular show, with every bird imaginable in the air, on the water and around us. Sir Julian was amazed.

The jheel disappeared when the Najafgarh drain was cleaned and made to carry water from Haryana and Punjab to the Yamuna.

I discovered another jheel at Sultanpur nearby, reached, then with difficulty, by a road wrecked by floodwaters; this was where the waterbirds had moved. The jheel was open water, without the islands and trees that were later added. I loved Sultanpur and the drive down the quiet country road from Mehrauli to Gurgaon, then a small but crowded town. On the rough road to Sultanpur, one day I spotted nesting blue-cheeked bee-eaters, thereby adding them to the Delhi list.

In 1969, Salím Ali, Sir Peter Scott, and other famous ornithologists were present at the IUCN Congress in Delhi, I took them to Sultanpur where they were amazed at the scene. Peter asked me if the jheel was protected. I said no, and subsequently told Indira Gandhi (then Prime Minister) about Sultanpur's wonders. She immediately asked Haryana's Chief Minister to declare it a sanctuary. She asked me to take her there, but, at the last moment she could not go. Ironically, in 1977, she was held in the newly-built rest-house there after her arrest and did see the jheel and its birds.

The Sultanpur Bird Sanctuary was inaugurated in 1972, after I had left India and joined WWF International in Switzerland, but during visits to India in the following years I was able to enjoy Sultanpur.

## How I Became a Birder

In 1953, Reuters sent me to cover the British Everest Expedition, when Edmund Hillary and Tenzing Norgay became the first to reach the summit. I was the lone reporter at the foot of Everest when the climbers came down and I got the first interviews with Hillary and Tenzing. A runner took a week to take the interviews to Kathmandu, from where they were sent to London to be published around the world.

It was on the two-week trek to Everest from Kathmandu that I became aware of birds. Having been brought up in a London suburb, I had paid little attention to them. But one day, as I rested during the trek, a large black bird sailed past me. I pulled out a book about the hill birds by someone named Salím Ali; it had been given to me by General Harold Williams, an Indian army engineer, mountaineer and birder, when helping to prepare my expedition in Delhi. On the cover was the large black bird, a Himalayan black eagle. Recognising that magnificent bird was the first step towards me becoming a birder.

As I continued the trek, I saw more eagles and many colourful birds. Most memorable was a flock of small birds; some largely red, and others yellow; a wonderful sight. Book out again, I found that they were scarlet minivets, as the males have brilliant scarlet wing, tail and breast feathers. The females were yellow. Seeing a brilliantly coloured monal pheasant flash through the bush was another great moment.

I spent two months in the Himalayas, much of the time at the Thyangboche Monastery, from where I had a magnificent view of Everest. I saw many bird species, including pheasants and the impressive bearded vulture, but had to concentrate on my job.

From the cool air of the Himalayas, I returned to a roasting Delhi, where my fellow-reporter, Adrienne Farrell, was based. It had been her idea that Reuters should send a reporter to Everest, something not done before. She helped organise my expedition and helped to get me a visa to Nepal. Some months later we were married and, in 1954, I joined Adrienne in Delhi as Reuters correspondent for India and Nepal.

I met General Williams again and told him about my adventures among the hill birds. One day, he said that Salím

Ali, the author of the book on hill birds, was coming to Delhi. He invited us to join them at Okhla, where he had betted Salím that you could see sixty bird species before breakfast.

In the presence of the great ornithologist, Adrienne and I expected to have to lie silently in the bushes to spot birds. Far from it; Salím turned out to be a very friendly, chatty man and we strolled by the river and through the bushes, while he and General Williams noted the birds sighted. Salím pointed to a long-legged bird in the water and told us it was a 'spotted sandpiper', so called because we had spotted it! It was one of the many little jokes that we were to hear from the great man. General Williams won his bet; the list reached sixty-eight in two hours, and then we had breakfast.

Salím came to Delhi again some months later on his way to Bharatpur, then known for its big duck shoots, and took us with him. We stayed with the Maharajah of Bharatpur, who became another good friend with whom we spent many later visits.

The huge mass of nesting waterbirds in the Ghana, (which later became the Keoladeo Sanctuary and then National Park), was stunning.

Salím's mission on this occasion was to ring young open-bill storks. We went with him in a boat among trees weighed down by nesting storks, egrets, cormorants and darters. Leaving our first baby in a carrycot on the bank, we paddled up to the birds, who became wildly excited. Salím reached out to grab the young storks' legs. The frightened birds exuded a black liquid over us, but Salím managed to ring them. Months later, he told us that some had been found fifty miles away.

Adrienne and I also accompanied Julian Huxley and his wife to Bharatpur, where he saw more than one-hundred birds in a day for the first time in his life, among them a small group of Siberian cranes that had just returned for the first time in twenty years. He wrote to me later, saying, 'I shall never forget our wonderful bird day!'

Following the surprise visit of those few Siberian cranes, more came during the 1960s. In 1968, I counted over eighty and photographed a group of fifteen of them. The Maharajah was still inviting friends for duck shoots. When the shooting began, the cranes would take off and glide overhead, making their plaintive calls, then drift down to feed again when the shooting ended.

Sadly, their numbers dwindled from the 1970s, and in November 2007, only a single crane arrived at Bharatpur—the last. It was thought that many were lost when passing through Afghanistan and Pakistan. A few cranes from their group, which nest by the Ob River, east of the Ural Mountains in Russia, still visit Iran, but the group is virtually extinct. The crane survives, however, with about two thousand in an eastern group that nests in Siberian Yakutsk, and winters in China.

There were a few people around the Ghana and we were able to cruise around in our car, leaving it to walk along the bunds, and to paddle around in my inflatable canoe.

Apart from the many birds, there were herds of deer and blackbuck antelopes, and twice I saw leopards. On one occasion I saw a cat crossing water on a fallen tree. At the time I did not know what it was, until years later, when I had become involved in wild cats, I realised that it was a fishing cat that was seldom seen in the Ghana.

## Vultures and Birds of Prey in Delhi

The Delhi sky was always full of vultures; some nested in trees in Janpath, despite the traffic, and there were fruit bats in adjoining trees. Rubbish dumps were surprisingly good birding sites! One could spot vultures, along with eagles, buzzards, lesser adjutants and storks, and many others.

In 1968–69, a Russian ornithologist, Vladimir Galushin, walked the Delhi streets every morning, recording nests of birds of prey. His published paper reported that there were about three thousand nesting pairs of birds of prey in Delhi, of which eighty-three percent were black kites. There were about four hundred pairs of large vultures.

The kites were everywhere, and you had to be careful if you had any food on an open-air table or even in the hand—they could swoop and fly away with it.

I twice picked up young kites that had fallen from nests. I kept them in the bathroom where they perched on water pipes. Visitors got quite a shock when they entered and found themselves observed by beady eyes. When they were fit to fly, I released the kites on the roof. They were surrounded at once by others anxious to inspect the new arrivals.

A friend who had an apartment by Lodi Gardens had a vulture nest close to his balcony. Early in the 1990s, he told me that Delhi's vultures were disappearing and no one knew why. I could scarcely believe it. We now know that the white-backed, slender-billed and long-billed vultures were dying after eating carcasses of livestock treated with the veterinary drug, Diclofenac. Despite a government ban, Diclofenac is still available and widely used, compromising efforts to restore these valuable birds.

## White-headed Yellow Wagtail

On a Sunday outing, in April 1965, I came across a procession of yellow wagtails alongside the Agra canal. I noticed that one had a white head and I assumed it must be an aberrant yellow-headed wagtail. But when I consulted the *Fauna of British India*, I found that the white-headed wagtail (*Motacilla flava leucocephala)* existed. The only previous record in India of this wagtail, according to Stuart Baker and Ripley (*Synopsis of the Birds of India and Pakistan*), was the one shot by Whistler on 3 May 1913, in Jhelum District, West Punjab. Since my sighting, I have only heard of one possible sighting of the wagtail, near Sonipat in 2003.

## A Day's Worth of Delhi Birds

When birding around Delhi we often recorded more than one hundred species in a day, and I began to think of how many birds one could see. I reckoned that it should be possible to top 150. The day was constantly put off until, on 1 March 1970, I awoke with the realisation that I was leaving India in July, the winter was past, and the chance might be lost forever.

As I left the bedroom, our resident house-sparrow sped across the living room to feed its nestlings on top of the almirah. Before I was in the car I had the house crow, green parakeet, common and brahminy mynahs and the black kite. As I turned down Prithviraj Road, heading for Mehrauli, blossom-headed parakeets flew alongside.

The first halt was at Mehrauli, where the dry, stony landscape, the rocks and the ruins produced some twenty more species, including the rufous-fronted wren warbler, the blue rock-thrush, brown rock-chat, yellow-throated sparrow and dusky crag martin.

I went on to Gurgaon, noting pale harrier, white-necked stock, white-eyed buzzard and steppe eagle, among others, on the way. From Gurgaon, I turned west, taking the old Farrukhnagar Road via Dhankot to Sultanpur jheel. Along the road I had to stop to write down the birds I had seen whenever they were becoming too many to remember.

At Sultanpur jheel the flocks of rosy pastors and flamingos were unmistakable and I sat down happily under a shady tree, with a telescope, to work over the various species of ducks, geese, waders, herons, storks and many more. By lunchtime, my list was going well at eighty-seven.

I went back to Gurgaon and took the road to Palam, crossed my morning route at Mehrauli, going on past Tughlakhabad to Mathura Road, adding to my list. From Madanpur a road ran down to the river at a point where market gardens ended, south of Okhla. This was a good place to pick up species, such as terns, striated weaver, pied mynah, purple gallinule and, as a bonus, a spotted dove, which was uncommon in the Delhi area at that time.

My plan to follow the cart track by the market gardens to Okhla, which could be very productive, was foiled by some earthworks and I had to speed round by the Mathura Road. I was now conscious that I had not seen the pied kingfisher, which I had considered one of the easiest to find. Surely, at Okhla . . . No, not for me that day.

A look at the ridge as the sun set yielded little, except one 'chuck', immediately noted as a nightjar. But no more 'chucks' followed, and I reluctantly crossed it off my list as uncertain.

It was dark passing through Chanakyapuri, but I paused at the crossroads near the American Embassy. I shone my spotlight into a tree—one of my spotted owlet friends did not let me down. It was at its nightly post.

My leap from bed that morning had not been as the first light of day spread over Delhi. It was 9 a.m. when I set forth – a shameful time for a birdwatcher. One claimed the right to a full 24 hours for my count, giving me until 9 a.m. next morning. Now I was up with the dawn, with a prepared list of species to get, and raced to the zoo. Not cheating! Delhi zoo attracted a fine selection of wild birds, and I was able to add several, including stone curlew, large-pied wagtail, night heron, coucal, and white-breasted waterhen. I was up to 141.

A visit to the Ridge again produced the golden-backed woodpecker, woodshrike and white-cheeked bulbul—144. The minutes were ticking away. I was desperate. My garden should still have something. It did. I ticked off the magpie robin, and as the second hand nudged up to 9 a.m., I closed with the red-whiskered bulbul.

I was four short of my minimum 150 target. But I was not depressed. It had been an exhilarating chase, and I don't think anyone would say 146 represents a bad day's birding anywhere in the world.

In retrospect, it seemed ridiculous not to have seen such common Delhi birds as the darter, pied kingfisher and white-eye, and even the coppersmith, which regularly nested in my garden. On the other hand, species such as the spotted dove and pale harrier were not to be expected, and so it probably worked out about right in the end. Even so, I am sure that the 150 mark could be reached reasonably easily, and perhaps pushed above 160, especially with more than one pair of eyes working together. In 2003, Kanwar B. Singh recorded 163 species in a day.

## Kashmir and the Pheasant-tailed Jaçana

During the hot weather, we would spend two or three weeks in Kashmir, which was a birder's heaven. We would get a houseboat, and be towed through Srinagar and up the Sind river to Shadipur. I was lucky to have the help of a skilled shikari, Sultana, who had worked for Salím Ali. He found nests and built hides in which I sat for hours to get good shots of birds at their nests. They were some of the happiest times of my life.

There is no time or space to tell stories of my many adventures in Kashmir, but one was special. I had tried many times to photograph pheasant-tailed jaçanas, particularly on the nest, without success. But one day, Sultana moved my hide slowly to about five metres from a nest with eggs, and the jaçana was returning. I quietly got into the hide, and a few minutes later the jaçana was back again, allowing me to get excellent photos. When I began to pack up, I noticed that the bird was pulling one of its eggs into the water. This was a great moment, because jaçanas were known to move their eggs to a new nest, but no one was heard to have seen it happen, let alone photograph it.

I set up the camera again and focused on the jaçana, which was moving backwards on its big, spindly feet, tapping the egg along with its bill. It took it to a new nest it had built about two metres further away and pulled it on. Then it returned three times to collect the other eggs.

I was wildly excited, but I had a big problem with my specialised camera. To focus on where the bird was likely to be with the floating egg involved several time-consuming adjustments. Nevertheless, I managed to get half a dozen shots, the first known of this remarkable bird behaviour.

## Sundarbans and the Goliath Heron

During a visit to India in 1974, I was in the Sundarbans, hoping to see tigers. Early one morning, a large heron rose from the water ahead of my boat. It was clearly a Goliath heron, an African species, but sometimes seen on the western shores of India. From records I found that Goliath herons had appeared in the Calcutta market in 1845–46, having come, almost certainly, from the Sundarbans. I later found that the Goliath heron had last been recorded in 1925 in the Khulna Sundarbans (now in Bangladesh), only a few miles from where I saw it. There have been several sightings since mine and I think it has probably not been noticed in the past because few, if any, visiting birders knew this African bird.

## Jerdon's Courser

Jerdon's courser was first described in the mid-nineteenth century by T.C. Jerdon, a Civil Surgeon in Nellore, not far from Cuddapah, in Andhra Pradesh. Unlike the common courser, which has a plain breast, Jerdon's courser has two white bands separated by black. Although there were occasional reports up to 1900, nothing was heard after that, and attempts to see if it still existed failed. In 1985, the Bombay Natural History Society (BNHS) sent ornithologist Bharat Bushan to interview village people in the Cuddapah area. The clue he had was that Jerdon reported receiving courser specimens on the same dates that he got some of the yellow-throated bulbul. Bharat reasoned that both birds might be found in the same place, and so he looked for the bulbul and began talking to local people about the courser. When they were shown pictures many said they knew it. Bharat now learned that Jerdon's courser was active at night, like two-banded coursers in Africa, and quite different from the common Indian courser.

A local hunter named Chinn Aitann from Reddy Palle village, caught one for Bharat. Unfortunately, it died before Salím arrived to see it. He was photographed holding the dead Jerdon's courser, at least happy that the species still existed.

On a visit to southern India, BNHS's J.C. Daniel and I decided to try to see the courser. We met Bharat at Cuddapah, and hurried to Reddy Palle village. As soon as it was getting dark we headed off with Aitann for the area where he knew Jerdon's courser existed. Because it is a night bird, it is exceedingly difficult to find, but we were lucky to have a moonless night, which Bharat said would be the best time because the courser would not see us first and move away.

Aitann had a powerful spotlight and a loud buzzer, powered by a motor-cycle battery. With two of us following in Indian file, he walked through open scrub, the buzzer muffling our footsteps while he swung the spotlight beam around in search of the mystery bird. We walked around for an hour or so without success. J.C. remarked that it was like looking for a needle in a haystack.

After supper in the village, we set off to another potential area. Bright stars provided a useful amount of light. Round and round we marched silently behind Aitann. There was a false alarm when the beam fell on a lapwing. Black-naped hares scuttled into the bushes. After two hours, we headed back to our jeep, but still searching on the way. As we came round a bush, Aitann suddenly gestured to the right. There it was: Jerdon's two-banded courser illuminated! It stood stock still, dazzled by the light and confused by the buzzer. I shot a picture, but the bird was standing with its back to me – not a satisfactory pose.

Aitann moved round to the right with the spotlight. The bird kept its back to the light, and became broadside on to me. I laid down and slowly crept close, snapping pictures. When I had half a dozen, we went on to our jeep, feeling very satisfied.

After days of excited expectation came disappointment. Although earlier photos were on the film, the courser photos were missing. It occurred to me that I had seen through the viewfinder the bird flinch at the flash; that indicated that the camera blind and shutter had not worked. The batteries must have run down as I walked for several hours with the camera switched on, ready for swift action. There are no regrets though. I have wonderful images in my head of Jerdon's two-banded courser.

## A Reminder of India

We left India in 1970 and moved to Switzerland, where I became WWF International's Director of Information. On a morning walk one day, I was astonished to see a hoopoe, an old friend from India, standing on the road. I found out that hoopoes visited Europe in the summer, but shortly after I heard that they had ceased to visit our part of Switzerland. Twenty years later, I was amazed to hear a loud 'poop-poop-poop' and saw a hoopoe again. They had returned, and came frequently to our garden; one even walked along a windowsill as I was sitting inside at my desk.

And it was not the only bird that returned at the time. I spotted a wryneck on the top of one of our trees. I had first seen one by the Najafgarh jheel, and been amused by its wonderful feather pattern. Best of all, the wrynecks settled in my nest boxes. Summers also brought some black kites to our area . . . bringing a little bit of India to my home.

# Where Tigers Swim

*BITTU SAHGAL*

*Bittu Sahgal's association with the Sundarbans goes back to his childhood. You could say these mangrove forests nurtured his passion for the wilds. This evocatively written piece on the Sundarbans, plainly reflects the author's fascination for this mystical realm of the tiger. Sahgal gave up his 'secure' job of an advertising executive to set up, in 1981, India's only wildlife magazine. As editor of* Sanctuary Asia *and founder editor of* Sanctuary Cub, *Sahgal has been closely involved with several national environmental and wildlife campaigns. He is also the author of several books, including* The Sundarbans Inheritance. *His columns on environmental and developmental issues appear in a number of publications in India. The cause he is most identified with is the one that seeks to save the tiger from extinction. He is also the founder of 'Kids for Tigers', an education programme in schools across India, aimed at increasing children's awareness about the nation's biodiversity. Sahgal's eloquent outspokenness has been the voice of India's beleaguered wildlife, and has waged a war against ill-planned development projects and government policies.*

January 2001. It is three in the afternoon and a brisk breeze whips my hair as I stand behind the prow of the Project Tiger patrol boat. I am making my way along the blue-green waters of the Netidhopani river in the Sundarbans Tiger Reserve, having chartered the day's course on a large map a few minutes earlier. It can get surprisingly bright on the water in the Sundarbans; even with sunshades on, the river's shimmer has me squinting. Happy to be alive, I see a dragonfly and a common wanderer butterfly navigate the strong wind to bisect the trajectory of our boat, 100 metres from shore. Pulling on a windcheater against the cold, I marvel at the magic of nature that gifts such fragile creatures with amazing flying capabilities.

About 250 metres ahead of our vessel, I spot a floating log. We are moving against the current about 30 metres from shore, I watch the log in a disinterested way, waiting for it to drift closer to our boat. That never happens. Instead, I begin to notice that it is moving at a 90 degree angle to us, and to the powerful current. Strange! At a distance of 150 metres, I peer through my binoculars and see a small round shape – certainly not a log. It takes me a full ten seconds to realise that a childhood dream has come true. I am in the Sundarbans, and there before me, in flesh and blood, is a wild tiger.

No one sees tigers in the Sundarbans. Everyone knows you come here for the experience, or to birdwatch, or just to escape urbania. Yet, against all probability, there she is. The cat's head, silhouetted and dark like some ancient god, is to our left perhaps 500 metres from the far shore. As we draw nearer, I can see her ears twitching. When she turns her head to stare at our boat,

I am struck by the yellow of her beautiful eyes. She is headed straight for the far bank but then, to my utter surprise, she turns and begins to swim back in the direction she came from.

Remorse now takes the place of the unadulterated joy I had just experienced on seeing the cat. How much energy has that cat already expended swimming against the powerful current? And I, who find real meaning in life only when serving the tiger, have disturbed and forced it to do just the opposite of what it had wanted.

Everyone is now on deck and there is consternation and excitement. I shout harsh instructions to the boatman to maintain a distance of at least 30 metres from the cat, and yell at him not to cut off her path to 'get a better look.' But the cat has other ideas. As our boat comes to a near-halt, it actually begins to swim back towards us with the current! She approaches as close as ten metres to our left, glancing up at us just once before heading for the shore from behind our vessel.

Tigers are very powerful swimmers. I can imagine her huge, paddle-like paws propelling her forward underwater. Her heart must be fit to burst from the exertion and anxiety. Effectively avoiding a second Project Tiger vessel positioned between our boat and the shore, she heads for the mudbank. Great paws touching earth, the tigress struggles momentarily in the slippery mud, and then bounds, tail up (which is how I, with my ringside view and binoculars, was able to conclude she was a she!) into the mangroves and is swallowed by the emerald forest.

The whole episode takes no more than three or four minutes, during which time I am granted momentary access into the life of one of the world's most secretive, most threatened predators. I have seen tigers in the wild scores of times across India, but for some reason that I cannot quite explain, this experience leaves me marked for life.

I have always known that the tiger was the keeper of the swamps. It will forever remain my master.

## Experiencing the Inheritance

Like nearly everyone who visits the Sundarbans Tiger Reserve, I began my trip at Sonakhali near the Matla river. I then went past Gosaba to reach Sajnekhali, at the confluence of the Pirkhali and Gomti rivers. Here, I took a quick walk through the orientation centre, and an even quicker climb up to the watchtower before boarding the Project Tiger patrol boat that was to be my home for the next few days. We cast off late in the afternoon and ever so often, we would pull as close to the shore as the mud would allow, getting a better look at wild boar digging for roots and chital and mud-caked macaques gorging on the fruit of keora trees. Gopal Tanti, assistant research officer with the Sundarbans Tiger Reserve casually mentioned that he had even seen fish eating fallen keora fruit.

As we traversed 'his' turf, he pointed out other plants such as *baen* and *genwa* and Oryza grasses – foods that sustain the Sundarbans web of life.

The Sundarbans is a birder's paradise and before daylight faded, I found myself identifying birds, comparing their beaks with the foods they sought. Curlews and whimbrels dug deep into the mud for crustaceans, sandpipers picked off smaller creatures from closer to the surface, brown-winged kingfishers waited patiently for a fish or crab to come within striking distance before swooping down on them like multi-coloured stealth bombers.

On slick mudbanks that melt like chocolate into the water, crocodiles, monitor lizards, mudskippers and fiddler crabs revealed themselves from time to time, like so many 'earth-jewels'. A snake painstakingly made its way towards an assemblage of mudskippers, but was thwarted at the very last moment when the fish, specially adapted for locomotion on land, darted away.

This utterly fragile, strange and magical ecosystem is geologically new and still evolving. Rivers and tides circulate nutrients like a chef might a great soup, with nothing wasted, as living creatures join the benthic flora in metabolising everything organic.

I discover that even the air is thick with drama as the sun begins to set. Above me, competing with swifts for the bounty of an insect-stocked sky, pigmy pipistrelles, *Pipistrellus mimus*, hawk flying food on the wing. Clearly, all is well with the world as darkness descends on Ghazikhali where we drop anchor for the night.

## Into Tigerland

Morning breaks to the sound of birdsong and an incoming tide slapping against the hull of our boat. Daylight creeps up on us and we pull anchor to head slowly on toward Bhagwan Bharani, stopping frequently with engines off to listen to the swamps.

At the Bidya Matla river intersection, I ask that the boat be halted while I photograph a white marker board on the north bank displaying the legend: 'International Steamer Channel'. It took ten months of intense lobbying, threats of exposés and court cases, plus a heated campaign in the media to get the project rejected by India's Central Ministry of Environment and Forests on environmental grounds. If it were ever to be built at some future date (a possibility we must contend with) the massive dredging alone would irreversibly alter the ecology of the swamps. On top of this, the inky blackness so crucial to the nocturnal ecology of the Sundarbans would be shattered by powerful lights from new jetties and landing stations. The throb of vessel after smoke-belching vessel would effectively rob the swamps of the silence, calm and tranquillity that characterise the tiger's abode.

In an ideal world, such jagged thoughts should never interrupt anyone's Sundarbans experience. More to my liking was the morning of 22 November 1999, when I woke at 5.15 a.m. in the Ghazikhali creek. I remember clearly how cold and dark it was, and how it felt like I could reach up and touch Venus and the millions of stars in whose light the narrow creek was illuminated like an unreal film set. By 5.30 a.m., collared doves had begun their guttural calls and the horizon had begun to lighten. By six, we set sail for Haldibari as a veritable avian orchestra of red junglefowl, eurasian curlews and common sandpipers broke out. Flock after flock of curlews and whimbrels flew low over the water, passing our boat only metres from herds of chital that gorged unafraid on the leaf bounty of the muddy swamp in the company of wild boar.

Half an hour later, we docked at the Haldibari Camp jetty and walked through a net-protected walkway to inspect a flotilla of fishing boats. Laden with Xylocarpus logs, the boats had been confiscated from wood poachers by the Forest Department. There are almost three-hundred-thousand people who scour the Sundarbans swamps to eke out a living each day, and some clearly are no longer satisfied with farming or fish. At this rate the forest will soon vanish, I thought darkly; sold to the highest bidder.

A deltaic swatch of low-lying mud and silt, the Sundarbans is a tropical estuarine swamp forest that harbours as many as sixty-five mangrove plant species, making it the most biodiverse mangrove forest in the world. Nutrients pour into this 'food factory' from all sides as flood waters from both the Ganges and the Brahmaputra mix and merge with the southern ocean tides to carve ever-shifting creeks and channels—the veins and arteries of the Sundarbans.

Nature respects no international boundary; nor do its wards. Tigers swim easily between Bangladesh and India using the powerful Harinbhanga, Raimangal and Kalindi rivers as passageways in their eternal search for food. Humans are not really welcome in the Sundarbans and life can be hard and very dangerous for them unless, of course, they happen to be travelling in the comfort of tourist vessels. Little wonder that human settlements exist only in the northern fringes where a marriage of solid ground and man-made dykes keep the tides tenuously at bay. However, though humans are not settled here, they pour into the swamps when the weather allows. This sets up a conflict of interest that ends up as a no-win situation in which humans, and tigers die.

## Wizards of Ooze

What a forest. What an incredible aquatic canvas for life. Away from human eyes, molluscs, worms, crustaceans and insects of all descriptions slime their way through the ooze. Eels, snakes, river terrapins, five marine turtles (olive ridley, green, hawksbill, leatherback and loggerhead) plus Gangetic and Irrawaddy dolphins live out silent lives, even as they micro-manage their muddy, aquatic domain to keep it productive. The Southwest monsoon showers the Sundarbans with pure, life-giving water, encouraging large heronries to form. As winter descends, millions of migratory waterfowl from the trans-Himalaya arrive to gorge on the bounty of the swamps. Crabs, snakes, butterflies and bees permanently sweep through the mangroves, mudflats and outlying sandy beaches sifting for food that arrives like manna from heaven-sent tides.

The tide is the heartbeat of the swamps, the rhythm of the Sundarbans. Tides govern the life of virtually every living creature that seeks sustenance from this aquatic paradise, from beetles and crabs, to the tigers in whose name all is protected.

## Bad Boys of the Swamps?

By some estimates, each day, depending on the phase of the moon, around thirty percent of the entire land area of the Sundarbans is submerged by tides ranging from one to almost six metres. This forces tigers, wild boar, monkeys and all other land-living creatures to crowd together into the greatly-reduced land area. Into this thickly-forested zone pour fisherfolk, honey gatherers and woodcutters who can only access the innermost creeks during high tide. When man enters a tide-shrunken, overgrown forest with just a few metres of visibility, a surprise encounter with a tiger is entirely possible. In such circumstances, the tiger may kill the human, not necessarily to eat him, but out of startled self-defence, or fear.

Hours later, when the body has been consumed by a host of scavengers, or perhaps even another passing tiger (all tigers will scavenge when they can), the automatic presumption is that a man-eater has struck, yet again. This perception that all tigers in the Sundarbans are man-eaters has been reinforced down the ages through myths and legends that gained credibility by very public accounts of genuine man-eating incidents. So, how should we label the vast majority of such tragic deaths? Man-eating? Or, man-killing?

I asked the late Kailash Sankhala, first director of Project Tiger, this question in 1981 and he replied, 'The Sundarbans tigers have an undeserved reputation. If all the Sundarbans tigers were habitual man-eaters, as is the popular misconception, we would see something like two or three thousand people killed and eaten each year between India and Bangladesh. That humans do not constitute a preferred food base for tigers is best demonstrated by the fact that even though it is capable of swimming three or four-kilometre wide rivers, the Sundarbans tiger seldom ventures out of its forest confines. On the other hand, it is the people that enter its domain and then, whether they die of snake bite, crocodile attack, or are murdered by another fisherman to whom they had lent money (not entirely unheard of!), the tiger is inevitably blamed.'

Kailash Sankhala died in 1994, but I can still feel his anguish at the persistent slander that has straddled the Sundarbans tiger with its man-eating label. Though no one should be foolish enough to imagine that a walk in the Sundarbans is as safe as a casual stroll through a backyard garden, the sheer number of people living in and traversing the Sundarbans swamps on foot and in shallow boats places the number of actual man-eating incidents in the category of 'statistically insignificant.'

What Sankhala said flies in the face of the fabulously colourful myths and legends of the Sundarbans. In any carnivore-inhabited forest in the country, a few individual cats can turn 'bad' and these animals are the ones that cause the entire pool of carnivores to be tarred with the 'man-eater' brush.

Be that as it may, the inherent human fear of the tiger does serve a useful purpose. 'Billy' Arjan Singh, one of the tiger's most ardent defenders, underscored this when he said: 'It is the fear of the tiger that has kept the Sundarbans comparatively inviolate. His disappearance would presage large-scale incursions of honey collectors and hunter gatherers.'

## Isolation as Protection

Left to its own devises, nature does a good job of looking after itself. For aeons it has been inaccessibility, not protection that ensured the survival of the Sundarbans' ecosystem and its wildlife. That some parts of the once-extensive swamps are still intact is tribute to the self-defence and auto-repair mechanisms of nature, not the wisdom or intent of *Homo sapiens.*

In days gone by, generations of settlers tried to 'tame' these forbidding swamps in relays. Hacking the Sundarbans was not merely considered brave, but the patriotic duty of citizens. It was such single-minded devotion to destruction that gave rise to legendary men such as Pir Mubarra Ghazi, who in the seventeenth century, turned vast parcels of the Sundarbans jungle to human use in the twenty-four Parganas.

From pirates in the pre-Moghul age, to the British and eventually the officials of free India and Bangladesh, it seems everyone hankered for a piece of the Sundarbans. The prime strategy was to create dykes called *bunds* high enough to prevent tide waters from 'invading' lands set aside for agriculture or homes. This was normally enough to kill the mangroves, which would then be cut, or burnt when dry. Valuable timber trees were always fair game. And thus, the deforestation saga continued for centuries. There was a time, for instance, that the Javan rhino, the water buffalo and the swamp deer found sustenance in the Sundarbans. No longer. Such animals needed a mix of habitats to survive and when the northern forests vanished, so did these animals, their departure hastened by uncontrolled hunting.

Lucrative incentives and official policies by successive governments in India and Bangladesh continue to encourage the destruction of the Sundarbans. Humans have wiped out around half the original spread of the Sundarbans. The bulk of this damage has been inflicted since the eighteenth century, when rice paddies, villages and townships pushed inexorably into the swamps. But the aggressive end-game is far from over. In an age when buzzwords like 'biodiversity conservation' and 'climate change' are the order of the day, and despite strong laws protecting the Sundarbans promulgated in both Bangladesh and India, it is these governments that most frequently violate the letter and spirit of their own protective laws.

Today, wherever *Homo sapiens* has succeeded in penetrating the swamps, deforestation, oil pollution, overfishing, reclamation and poaching have resulted. If it were mere paddy fields and townships we had to deal with, time and tide might eventually restore the balance of nature. India, however, seeks to build nuclear reactors and cut international steamer channels through this fragile biosphere. An astounding 'alternate energy' proposal to set up a small thermal plant fuelled by 'renewable' mangrove wood was mercifully rejected. Bangladesh, meanwhile, is being actively seduced by Shell Oil to allow oil and gas exploration in the Sundarbans.

Conservationists on both sides of the border have been fighting their battles in the arena of public opinion and in the law courts to prevent the 'opening up' of the Sundarbans. If they fail, if the isolation of the Sundarbans is even more widely breached, one of the world's richest marine nurseries will die. And in an era of galloping climate change, not only will *Panthera tigris* suffer, but millions of innocent humans will be exposed to more violent and more frequent cyclones and tidal surges.

Of course, it need not be this way. The tiger could become a rallying point, a compass to lead us away from our impending ecological doom.

## Save the Tiger, Save Ourselves

Scientists now know that functional mangrove ecosystems, coral reefs, seagrass beds, and inter-tidal mudflats are crucial to the moderation and control of global climate. Ironically, though the swamps help counter climate change, they could well prove to be one of its earliest victims. The tiger and all other denizens of the Sundarbans have adapted over the years to temperature variations that swing seasonally between 15.0 and 34.50 degree Celsius, and rains that fall between mid-June and September. How will the fluctuations beyond such ranges affect the food chain? Will palatable grass and tree species dwindle? Will the breeding biology of insects be thrown awry? Will a chain reaction of adversity set in faster than species can adapt? By some estimates, the seawater rise in the Sundarbans is currently 3.14 mm per annum, against a global mean average of 2.2 mm.

It is likely that this rate is going to accelerate. How long will it take for rising seas to take away denning sites of tigers, where mothers raise their young? Uncertainty prevails on this and almost every other front for the kingdom of the tiger.

In retrospect, the setting aside of 2,585 sq km of the Sundarbans swamps in 1973 was hugely providential. Though parts of the swamp forest had enjoyed *de jure* forest protection for quite a while, the *de facto* situation was that thousands of people came and went as they pleased. This badly stressed the Sundarbans' prodigious stock of fish, prawns and crabs, as thousands of boats entered the creeks, spread their fine mesh fishnets, hauled in what was valuable, and threw away what was not. How could the breeding potential of marine species of the Sundarbans not become seriously diminished? What is more, for reasons explained above, each year, perhaps over one hundred people used to lose their lives, reportedly to tigers. It was a vicious cycle with no winners.

## Independence for the Tiger

It took decades of patient effort and systematic policy implementation on the part of the West Bengal Forest Department to broker a fragile peace. Till 18 August 1947, the Sundarbans was managed by a single authority: the Sundarbans Division, headquartered at Khulna. Three days later on 21 August, everything changed. Independence from the British created East Pakistan (now, Bangladesh), dividing the administration of the Sundarbans with 4,262 sq km in the twenty-four Parganas in India in the charge of West Bengal.

Of this, 2,585 sq km was declared the Sundarbans Tiger Reserve on 23 December 1973, comprising 1,680 sq km of land and 905 sq km of water. The buffer zone, like a sort of organic shock absorber, was established to keep humans and animals away from each other. This was in line with Sankhala's strategy: 'Leave nature to its own devices. Do next to nothing . . . allow nothing to be done.'

Had such a policy been in place in the mid-1880s, perhaps a visitor to the Sundarbans today might have been able to see a Javan rhinoceros, *Rhinoceros sondaicus*, or a wild buffalo, or swamp deer, all of which are now extinct from the Sundarbans. In the event, the strategy of Project Tiger in the 1970s was a success. The tiger had gained its independence from humans, who had colonised its forests. Between the inhospitality of the jungle and the protectionist mission of a few farsighted humans, tigers and their tidal ecosystem gained a fresh lease of life.

The ancient Sundarbans inheritance was handed over, intact, to a new generation.

Excerpted from *The Sundarbans Inheritance*,
by Bittu Sahgal, Sumit Sen and Bikram Grewal
*Sanctury Asia*, 2007

# Day Eight

*VALMIK THAPAR*

*Valmik Thapar is the tiger's best known supporter. He has worked for over thirty years to save wild tigers, served on various government and international committees, anchored films, and authored well over a dozen books on the big cats. His love for the tiger was born, and nurtured, in Ranthambhore – a small, but amazingly rich tiger reserve in the shadow of a medieval fort in Rajasthan. The park inspired many a book by Thapar, including* The Secret Life of Tigers, *which recorded amazing revelations on the tiger's family life. Then came a phase when Thapar put down his pen – tigers were dying, edging towards extinction, and he lost heart. It was Ranthambhore, again, that soothed him; and even if tigers are as endangered today, this reserve gave him a window of hope. This extract from* Ranthambhore: Ten Days in the Tiger Fortress *describes the magic he witnessed, a treasure of tigers renewed when all had but been lost in despair. The following article, as the title explains, is his* Day Eight *at the Reserve.*

As we enter Ranthambhore, we get news of tigers in Gular Kui, the lower reaches of the fort, and I spend some time debating whether to go there, knowing full well that much of the tourist traffic would be around the tiger. We do end up going, only to find the mother, Machli and one of her cubs above a waterhole. They look as if they have eaten, and the remnants of their kill are in the grass. There are too many vehicles around; so we move off, intending to return later. When we do, we find fewer vehicles and both the tigers in the water.

The cub soon leaves the water and Machli continues to sit for twenty minutes, cooling off, while her cub seems restless to move. Then both the mother and the cub start the long walk. They move nearly four km on the road to Jogi Mahal. For one hour we follow, luckily the first in a long convoy of vehicles. The cub claws trees, marks the ground, scampers, tries to play with her mother, and is in a much better mood than the other day when they boxed it out. It's all to do with having a full stomach. I see Daulat Singh, the Ranger, approaching from the far side. The tigers continue their walk, passing a gate with tigers painted on it in folk style. They manoeuvre past cars and traffic on the main tarmac road to the park, passing by two stunned motorcycle riders. As they walk upwards, the cub pauses to mark a milestone; it says – Ranthambhore: 1 km. My son, Hamir, watches bemused as the mother and cub slide past our jeep. At the top of the hill, right below the ramparts of the fort, they pause and cross over the wall that leads to Jogi Mahal, which is also where we are supposed to have a cup of tea with the park director. It's been a superbly exciting morning and we get off at Jogi Mahal enveloped in contentment. We chat with the director and ranger on the balcony. Sanjna goes off to climb and sprawl on Hamir's favourite branch of the banyan tree. Peace descends, broken by occasional peacock alarm calls. It could be tigers a few hundred yards away. A few minutes later, I hear the pattering of deer hooves, and as I turn towards the sound I see a herd of spotted deer scampering through the banyan tree; at the same time I see Sanjna racing to the steps of Jogi Mahal with Hamir in her arms. Time stops. I move a few steps forward, and then witness the most unbelievable sight as one of the tigers—the dominant cub—jumps into the tree just where Sanjna and Hamir had been seconds earlier. Sanjna used her instinct and fortunately moved away from danger. This created space for a tiger to jump in. I must say, I was a bit nervous but there was no time to think. My dream had come true, and my camera clicked the first pictures ever in my life of a tiger under this ancient banyan tree; adrenalin flowed and the cub moved off. We were still excitedly discussing this amazing event when again, minutes later, a cheetal alarm call punctured our conversation and turned our attention back towards the tree where we saw the breathtaking sight of a tiger racing full speed under the tree after a cheetal fawn. I managed two shots before the tiger vanished. Our excitement was at its peak. Hamir didn't know what had happened. I was again in seventh heaven, or is there an eighth one?

Only once in the last thirty-three years, sometime in the 1980s, on waking up in the middle of the night and looking towards the banyan tree from my window, I had caught a glimpse of a tiger slipping by. But I never really knew whether it had actually happened or if it was a dream. Right now I was near hysterical with excitement, telling the park director that it was a dream come true for me. He must have thought I was mad. Suddenly, one of the jeep drivers said, 'Tiger coming back!' I rushed on foot to the corner of the tree even though the director tried to stop me. I knew it was now or never. And I watched the tigress retrace her steps calmly and slowly, walking past the branches and roots of what has to be one of the finest trees of its kind in India. I clicked carefully, moving a few paces with her, a few steps at a time. My heart was pounding with the banyan tree chase!

That afternoon when we returned, it was as memorable as ever, with tigers crossing within a few feet of us as they walked across the lake with the setting sun staring at us and pacing off down the road in front of us. All three cubs were around, as if they were getting ready to say farewell. We had seen so much of tigers that it was all coming out of every pore of our beings. And it was not just the sight but the sound as well, with lots of roaring, growling, and snarling. The sight of tigers merged with the sounds and even the smell – that strong musky odour that comes when you get really close to tigers. We left two tigers on the edge of the road and returned home.

I don't think I have ever had such an amazing eight days, and today had been particularly incredible. Though Daulat Singh was still going to take us out on the ninth day, I knew that the trip was over and today had been its culmination. We did a little 'jungling' around that evening with Hamir and slept out in the open under the stars. Before I went to sleep that night, my mind was racing with excitement. The unexpected had happened. I had now to put picture to paper. I had to bring out the essence of this very special window of time that Ranthambhore and its tigers had allowed me, and that too at a juncture when the tiger was facing its worst crisis in India.

Extracted from *Ranthambhore: 10 Days in the Tiger Fortress*,
Valmik Thapar, Oxford University Press, 2008

# Looking for Mermaids in the Indian Ocean

*HASMUKH HOSLO JIWA*

*With our concentration mainly on land animals, we know little of the wonders and the amazing diversity of life that flourish under the sea. One such creature is the dugong, the only sea mammal that lives solely on vegetation.*

*Hasmukh Hoslo Jiwa was first lured by the sirenians when he had a special encounter with a manatee, the dugong's closest living relative, off the Florida coast, launching him into a lifelong quest to work for the 'sirens of the sea'. Over the past six years, Hasmukh has been monitoring the dugongs off the islands of Andaman and Nicobar, working with indigenous people and the government for their conservation. He has also surveyed the aquatic mammal along the Indian coast, and worries for it's bleak fate. The dugong, he says, is teetering on the brink of extinction on the Indian shores.*

*Hasmukh is one of the founding members of Green Life Society, and concentrates his efforts towards generating employment for local youth and protecting the fragile environment of the Andamans by setting up plastic recycling plants. He earns his living as a photo-journalist for various magazines, and specialises as an underwater video/photographer.*

'There have been no *Inyabonye* (dugong) for a long time. I don't think they are here anymore,' remarked the Onge captain during our search for mermaids.

It was December 2003 – my first trip to Little Andaman Island in the Indian Ocean. I was headed to Dugong Creek, in Onge territory. One of the world's smallest indigenous groups, the Onge, live only in the Union Territory of the Andaman and Nicobar Islands. Receiving permission to conduct work there is nearly impossible, and it was only because I am the principal investigator for the GreenLife Society Dugong Project that I eventually got the okay to survey the area for a month. Needless to say, I was extremely excited about working in such a unique place with such fascinating people.

Dugongs are Sirenian, named after the Sirens of ancient Greek mythology. In Homer's *Odyssey*, Sirens were half-women, half-bird creatures that tried, with sweet songs of love, to lure Odysseus and his ship onto their island. Later, some authors confused Sirens with mermaids (mythical creatures described as half-women, half-fish), possibly because of their pectoral breasts, dexterous forelimbs, and fish-like tails. Eventually the scientific order, *Sirenia,* was named to classify the dugongs and manatees.

Dugongs are more closely related to elephants than to other marine mammals such as whales and dolphins, but their closest living aquatic relatives are the manatees. Another close relative was the Steller's sea cow, previously found in the northern Pacific. It was hunted to extinction in the 1700s by sealers for its meat.

Dugongs have whale-like flukes in place of the paddle-like manatee tails. They spend all their lives in salt water, where they feed on sea grasses. Like all other marine mammals, dugongs must surface to breathe, but unlike whales and dolphins, dugongs cannot hold their breath under water for very long. Dugongs are found on the southeast coast of Africa and west coast of Madagascar, north of the Arabian Peninsula, and east of the Philippines and Japan. They have disappeared from many parts of this broad range, and are under serious threat in most of the remaining sites.

In the 1950s, dugongs were common in the Union Territory of the Andaman and Nicobar Islands, but since then the population has drastically declined. Local tribes, namely, the Onge, the Andamanese, and the Nicobare, traditionally hunted dugongs with iron harpoons tied to boats. But none of these tribes, except the Andamanese of Strait Island, regularly practise this tradition now because of the time and effort required.

The Onge have been isolated on the Indian Ocean islands for the past 20,000 years. A hundred years ago, this tribe numbered about 1,000. When I arrived in their midst, the population was just ninety-five.

Onge is a word these people do not recognise. They call themselves *En-iregale*, meaning 'perfect man.' It was probably Lieutenant Colbrooke of the British Navy who, in 1790, first used the term Onge, and pronounced it Ungee. The Onge resemble African Pygmies in height (averaging a little over four feet) and facial characteristics.

For thousands of years, the Onge occupied the entire island of Little Andaman. Beginning in the 1880s and continuing through the 1970s, the British and Indian governments pushed them into settlements in the north and south of the island. In their place the governments settled Katchi (labourers) and introduced Andamanese tribes in the port area of Hut Bay. The Onge find themselves today in the same situation as the dugongs – facing extinction. And, the fates of both are linked.

After arriving in Port Blair, capital of the Union Territory, I nearly missed the boat to Little Andaman, where I was to stay at the Tribal Welfare Camp. Food and accommodation had been arranged. All I had to worry about was making sure my snorkelling and computer equipment worked.

The boat left Port Blair at precisely 6.30 a.m. I settled myself on a wood bench, and as I stared at the azure waters of the sea, my mind drifted back to how this had all started. Though I was always interested in creatures of the sea, my obsession with dugongs could be traced to an encounter with another sea-cow in the summer of 2001. I was in Florida, very lonely, with no friends, and hardly any money. I felt depressed, and decided to go snorkelling to shake away the feeling of despondency.

I entered the water, and as I went further into the sea, the water started getting murky. I figured I didn't stand a chance of 'seeing' anything, so I decided to turn around and go back. That is when I felt a presence, as though I was being observed. I looked up to see, and not one metre away – the Florida Manatee! Surprise would be an understatement. I had been trying to see this animal in the wild for years and years. And here he was, right now, in front of me.

What followed was quite unbelievable.

I reached out a tentative hand, and lightly scratched his head. He didn't move, so I got a bit bolder. I scratched his back like you would a dog's and he rolled over onto his stomach. Astounded, and thrilled by his reaction, I joined him as he proceeded to dive in the deep water. We swam together, shoulder-to-shoulder. I felt calm and at peace with the Manatee, I felt the purest essence of friendship, a positive energy, I can't explain the feeling more than that, as we swam. I lost all track of where I was, who I was. At that moment, I was in his world; I had lost my own identity.

I was jolted awake by the chanting of 'Hare Krishna', and found that there were many followers of the Hare Krishna movement on board. On enquiry, I discovered that the local people had invited them to come and pray for them. Somehow, that gave Little Andaman an ominous feel to it.

Eight hours later, we arrived at Hut Bay. Upon disembarking, I headed straight to the district magistrate's office to inform him of my arrival and to make arrangements for transportation to Dugong Creek. Having settled that, and after checking into the guest house, I headed to a small eatery. I got talking to the owner, Joy, and explained to him what I was doing. I showed him my dugong slide presentation. Soon, eight enthusiastic people had huddled around the laptop, and I had begun my first awareness programme. 'I want to help as much as I can. I have been living here all my life and never knew that it was this beautiful under water,' Joy promised.

The next day, Joy and I set off to find a fisherman to take us to Dugong Creek. Hut Bay is basically one road that connects the south and north. To the north, we found fishermen doing odd jobs around their boats. No one wanted to take us, so I decided to interview them. Having Joy with me made the fishermen relax, and I learned that all fifteen of them were familiar with the dugong. What was more surprising and shocking was that they all had eaten it. Two of the fishermen had spotted around one hundred dugongs in the northern part of Little Andaman three months previously. To be sure they weren't confusing dugongs with other marine mammals, I also showed them pictures of dolphins, but they distinguished them correctly.

Eventually, we persuaded a fisherman to ferry us. As his *doonghi* (boat) chugged through the murky, warm waters of serpentine mangrove-lined creeks flanked by nypa palm and rhizophora, saltwater crocodiles darted to and from the muddy banks. Before making our way out to the open sea, we had to wait for the tide to rise. It took an hour in open water to reach the mouth of Dugong Creek, and once again, we had to go with the tide to enter. I could understand why it had been so difficult to find someone to take us there. When we finally arrived, we were met on the jetty by an Onge boy, Jain, dressed in red shorts and an Andaman and Nicobar tourist T-shirt, and Ramnat, the camp security guard.

I was surprised to learn that the Onge have been named after Indian anthropologists and biologists and tribal welfare personnel who have worked there. When I inquired about their real names, the Onge captain told me that they did not have names before. They called one another 'father's sister's son' or 'brother's wife's sister,' and so on.

Early next morning, Ramnat escorted me to the first temporary village the Onge had made – Basti 1. The Onge did not like the accommodations the Indian government had built for them because the houses were too hot. They preferred to stay by the beach in shelters constructed out of small trees.

The majority of Onge adults were wearing some clothing, and the children were naked. My first glimpse of their way of life reminded me of some remote villages in Africa, where I had worked in the 1990s. I showed them photos of dugongs and observed their reactions. Their answers to my queries were mixed, but I put this down to their being cautious and reserved. I met a few of the youngsters, and we spent the rest of the day fishing and looking for crabs. Back at my quarters, an old wooden house, I found some spices and flour to make *chapattis* and cooked up a real feast, which I enjoyed with the children.

The next day, I snorkelled along the three miles of coast from my house to the Onge village; giant rays swam around me, and brilliant green beds of sea-grass looked like huge football fields intermingled with sea cucumbers and corals. Each afternoon, at around one o'clock, the sea cucumbers would start to feed, munching into the sand next to the sea-grass. Dugongs, however, remained elusive.

I had gotten off to a good start with the Onge. I made the children laugh, and this made the elders more comfortable. I also befriended all the dogs in the camp. The British introduced dogs to the Onge, who consider them part of their families because they assist in hunting for wild pigs. The dogs eat whatever the people do, and sleep in beds built for them in the huts.

I asked the village captain about dugongs, and he remarked he had not seen one for many years, but I knew he was being circumspect because other researchers had reported two young dugongs killed at Dugong Creek the previous summer. The Onge are exempt from the Wildlife Protection Act and may kill endangered species if they need food. It took a few days to build up trust among the people, but soon they invited me to hunt for dugongs at high tide during the full moon.

On the day of the hunt, I arrived at the village just before sunset. The mosquitoes and sand flies had decided I was supper, and even the usually effective neem oil did not deter their attacks. As usual, the children were curious about the foreigner in their midst and gathered around me. Their bodies were painted with white clay, and when I inquired, they pointed to one of the huts. Inside, at the back of the hut, one of the women was spreading the gooey substance all over a baby boy. They explained that when they cover themselves with clay, the mosquitoes do not bite. I encouraged the woman to put some on my face, and I applied the rest to my sore arms and legs. It worked! This is the same clay for which people pay $100 for a single application at spas around the world.

At 10.25 p.m., the Onge hunters motioned that it was time for the hunt. Though I was excited, I kept thinking about how I would react if they found a dugong, and whether I would try to stop them from killing it. I knew the Onge were hunting for food, but I was there to learn about and protect a rare species. Catching dugongs is no easy affair, as they are secretive and elusive. A successful hunter must have intimate knowledge of dugong behaviour, what they eat, their favourite feeding spots, the best tide for hunting, and the relationship between the tides and the phases of the moon. Historically, when the Onge population was higher, only a few men were allowed to hunt. With their numbers in decline, they are losing this skill, so I concluded that the chances of these men killing a dugong were slim.

The moon guided us as we pushed off in the *houri*, a primitive single-sided catamaran canoe. One Onge hunter stood in the bow, ready with a harpoon to strike, and another was at the stern, controlling the *houri*. The harpoon wielder, his eyes fixed on the water, never spoke or moved as we made transects, looking for movement or the shadow of a sea turtle or dugong. Two hours later, he suddenly gave a hand signal, and the boat turned sharply to the right, toward a spot where the sea-grass was dominated by *Thalassia hemprichii*, commonly called dugong grass. I could just make out a dugong feeding. I was exulted: this was my first sighting of a wild dugong! But at the same time I was gripped with a morbid horror: they were going to kill it; what could I do? The hunter recited some spells under his breath, to lure the animal closer. As he raised his harpoon, the boat creaked, and the dugong darted away in a swirl of sand . . . I was overwhelmed with a sense of relief, and happy to have seen my first wild dugong!

As we headed back to camp, I decided I must pursue another course of action to find dugongs – one that would not endanger them. So, I returned to Port Blair and met with the Deputy Inspector General (DIG) of the Coast Guard and the Chief Wildlife Warden. The DIG offered one of his ships, CGS *Lakshmi Bai*, to cover the northernmost area of Little Andaman, where a fisherman had spotted dugongs in Bulmila Creek. The ship's crew understood the importance of becoming more involved in environmental monitoring.

One day, while we were surveying in Dugong Creek, the weather began to change. We knew we had only a few hours before the outer edge of a cyclone would be upon us. We tried to reach Bulmila Creek for four consecutive days, but were beaten back by heavy winds and giant swells. With the weather against us, we sought shelter at Hut Bay. During our absence, an Onge child had died of high fever, bringing the population down to ninety-four.

I made plans to continue my study after the monsoon season. I hope that somehow we can help both the Onge and the dugong increase their numbers in these islands.

## Afterword

It's coming to my sixth year on the Andaman Islands. We lived through the Tsunami, the destruction it wrought delayed a lot of work that needed to be done after this initial survey. The administration also became more difficult with giving permissions and I decided to work in areas where permits weren't required.

In November 2007, a female dugong was killed around Neil Island. The tragedy is that this shameful episode was ignored by the Forest Department even though the carcass was sold openly in the island's market square. The dugong was caught by a fisherman, and according to some reports, it was still alive, when he mercilessly cut its head off and bought the pieces to be sold in the Neil Island market for fifty rupees a kilo (about one dollar).

She was a female, and her slaughter brought down the population of dugongs in Neil Island to six. Killing a female is akin to finishing a generation, for the dugong is a slow-reproducing mammal, with a calving period of three to seven years. At the current rate, where one dugong is killed every two years, there will be virtually no dugong left after five years.

In the Gulf of Mannar, the situation is even more desperate. During a week-long survey, we came across intestines of the dugongs strewn on the beach at Appa Island. In the past two years (2006–08) eight dugong deaths have been officially reported. The gulf with its abundant seagrass is ideal to support thousands of dugongs, yet indiscriminate hunting has put this animal on the brink of extinction. The history of dugong killing in the Gulf of Mannar is unchecked and unpunished, e.g. around 250 dugongs were killed in 1985 and a further 146 caught in nets in 1986. The chances this slow reproducing mammal will ever recover from such a massacre is very dim.

In January 2008, twelve people were arrested by police and wildlife rangers at a night-time seize operation, though it was accidental. The police suspected that the truck was smuggling arms, but they were transporting a dead dugong for consumption. This led to the first case pertaining to dugongs being brought before an Indian court.

*Circa* August 2008: I am on a train to the Gulf of Kutch, hoping to set up the first of three Dugong Monitoring Units (DMU). The task is to employ local fishermen to help its conservation and monitoring, and also develop a training programme to train forest rangers on how to become marine rangers.

The dugongs of India are in serious trouble because of the twin threats of hunting and habitat destruction. In the Gulf of Kutch, on one hand, the Gujarat government is receiving financial support from the World Bank for coral restoration and protection, and on the other hand, building 'minor' coal importing ports on the best coral areas that are financed by big business houses like Adani and Tata. Here, it seems multi-crore projects are more important than protecting areas under Marine Protected Parks.

In the Gulf of Mannar, the Sethusamudram project will disrupt the biosphere area of sea-grass, constant trenching of the canal system will deposit sediments onto the sea-grass. No one has studied the migratory routes of the dugong. So, it is anybody's guess what dredging for sea-routes will do to this rare mammal's habitat.

I have been asked many times why do I do this strange work, with this strange animal. And I remember the world that opened up to me with the first sea-cow I met and how we swam, and played together. We were friends, and I look after my friends when they are in trouble. It's as simple as that.

# Munzalas in the Mist: The Discovery of the Arunachal Macaque

CHARUDUTT MISHRA AND ANINDYA SINHA

*Charudutt Mishra is one of the founders of the Nature Conservation Foundation, and serves as the Science and Conservation Director of the Snow Leopard Trust. His work in the high altitudes of the Himalayas and Central Asia focuses on community-based conservation, research on wild carnivores, herbivores, indigenous peoples, and human-wildlife conflict. He works with local communities and governments to catalyse wildlife conservation. Anindya Sinha is a primatologist and is associated with the National Institute of Advanced Studies and the Nature Conservation Foundation. With a doctorate in Molecular Biology, Sinha has worked on diverse topics, including the social biology of wasps and the population genetics of primates. To their team is attributed, amongst the rarest events in natural history, the discovery of a new species of macaque in Northeast India. It merits mention that the last macaque species to be discovered was over a century ago. In today's grim scenario, with the rate of extinction at its peak, such stories give us hope.*

In a remote corner of western Arunachal Pradesh, sandwiched between the Kingdom of Bhutan and the People's Republic of China, it was another wet and misty monsoon afternoon. One of us was behind the wheels, while several pairs of eyes, including those of colleagues Aparajita Datta and M.D. Madhusudan, gazed intensely through the blanket of mist, desperately looking for signs of the road. Visibility was reduced to just a few metres. There were moments when even the last few visual references along the mountain road disappeared. Yet, we kept moving, pushed to rather unintelligent limits by feelings of anticipation and anxiety.

There was anticipation in the air because we had just started exploring the little-known high-altitude regions of Arunachal Pradesh, arguably India's richest region in terms of terrestrial biodiversity. There was immense excitement, as the biological wealth of these parts had hitherto been only poorly documented or explored. In a refreshing deviation from field experiments and statistical tests that are the bane of any field ecologist's life, in this forgotten corner of India all of us felt transported back a few centuries earlier, to the age of discovery. Emotions were strong, only instinct and driving experience, and indeed luck, embanked us from the Nyamjangchu River flowing several hundred metres below, rushing its way into Bhutan.

But we were also anxious. The anxiety stemmed from the nagging need to justify the time, the effort, and the society's resources that make field research and conservation possible. It is an anxiety that any scientist or conservationist constantly feels, particularly at the beginning of a project, before meaningful results start trickling in. That can take months, sometimes even years.

Suddenly, the mist cleared magically, and a small troop of equally magical monkeys ran across our path into the understorey. The vehicle screeched to a halt. Through our binoculars, the animals looked large and impressive, and they looked different from any other monkey we had ever seen. It was 19 August 2003, our first sighting of what would later come to be known to the world as the Arunachal macaque. This troop of four to five monkeys disappeared from our view as quickly as it had appeared, leaving us thrilled but also a little disappointed at not having been able to observe them at length.

I don't think the significance of the moment hit us then, but we realised that we were onto something important.

Yet, we were unsure.

Was it our imagination? Wishful thinking, perhaps? That these primates were unlike any others in the planet? A new species? It was just too remarkable, too inconceivable a notion – that a new species could be discovered in a land of a billion people, with its wild habitats shrinking.

In the weeks that followed, we were to sight eight more troops of this monkey. It took some effort though, as our biological expedition involved over 800 km of driving and more than 200 km of trekking and camping in slushy forests and meadows, often in wet sleeping bags and dripping tents. Throughout the expedition, we remained uncertain about what this primate was. Was it, for instance, a different-looking representative of the Assamese macaque that is reported to occur in this part of the country?

The expedition got over after a few weeks, and we headed back, still confused. But we soon got busy; we had our data to analyse, papers to publish, and reports to send to our funding agencies. In addition to this primate, we had recorded, during our expedition, a fascinating assemblage of high-altitude species, that included the snow leopard, bharal, Chinese goral, red panda and others. We had, in the process, also identified and mapped an important site for wildlife conservation in Arunachal Pradesh, where the state government is now trying to set up a biosphere reserve.

The secrets surrounding the identity and other aspects of this primate's life, however, kept nagging us. After just a few months, in April of 2004, the two of us found our way back to Arunachal Pradesh, to conduct more field observations on this mysterious monkey. Another 200 km were surveyed by road and 80 km on foot. We made detailed field-observations, and captured the monkey in photographs and videos. Then, in 2005, in a paper published along with Aparajita and Madhu in the *International Journal of Primatology*, we described this monkey as the Arunachal macaque, a species new to science.

This description of a new species of monkey from the Eastern Himalayas, with its characteristic short tail and distinctive facial markings, caused much excitement and generated much debate among scientists, conservationists, and people at large across the world. After all, it is not common for a species as large as the Arunachal macaque to have remained hidden and undiscovered in today's day and age. This happened to be the only new macaque to be discovered in over a century since the Pagai macaque was last described from Indonesia in 1903.

Indeed, ours wasn't a 'discovery' in the true sense, as the species had always been known to the local Monpa community who share its habitat. These monkeys have been in their neighbourhood for a long time, much before the sixth Dalai Lama was born in the region, or the celebrated Tawang monastery was built. The Monpa have known the Arunachal macaque from the time that they inhabited these lands and started cultivating their crops. The monkeys, as they have perhaps always done, even today cause damage to the crops of millets, wheat, buckwheat, and barley that are grown in the region. The Monpa even have a distinct name for this primate. The 'munzala', literally 'monkey of the deep forest', is the local name of the species in the Dirang Monpa dialect. Yet, the species had remained unknown to science. We described it scientifically and named it, giving it the official scientific name *Macaca munzala* in honour of the traditional knowledge of the Monpa people.

It was after almost one-and-a-half years of sighting our first troop of his monkey that we stumbled upon a specimen of this species that we could actually physically examine and measure: An adult male Arunachal macaque that had been killed by villagers when he entered a house, searching for food. We found it at the end of a cold day in the beginning of March 2005, in the remote village of Sokchen, close to the China border. Having spent the day searching for live troops, this was sudden and unexpected, and a rush of emotions took over as we looked at the inert primate. We felt sick in our hearts to see such a fine animal dying before its time. For several moments, we stood there, disoriented, watching its lifeless body, trying to make sense of the situation while simultaneously attempting conversation with a handful of villagers who looked confused by our seemingly strange interest.

Over the next few minutes, the mist, this time in our heads rather than in the air, slowly cleared up. Scientific curiosity and cold rationality took over. This was, after all, the first specimen of the Arunachal macaque that would ever become available to the scientific world. Earlier, while describing the new species, because of ethical reasons, we had deviated from the standard practice of sacrificing individual specimens while naming a new species, and had been among the first people to report the discovery of a mammalian species on the basis of photographs alone. We realised that we had to rush with the specimen to the Itanagar Zoo, several hundred mountainous kilometres away, where we would treat the specimen, preserve its skin and bones, measure them, and deposit them at a museum.

The leopard is a shy, se
agile creature—rare
in the forest. It i
increasingly threate
illegal trade of its sk
bones, and by c

Kalyan Varma

Jayanth Sharma

e Gir National Park in Gujarat is the only home of the Asiatic lion.

gongs are also referred to as sea cows, perhaps because their diet consists mainly of grass.

The Asiatic wild dogs, or dholes, are skilled hunters.

Vivek Sinha

Sloth bears are hunted for their gall bladders, and face the constant pressure of deforestation.

This particular elephant, or 'The Mating Tusker', was electrocuted – a victim of conflict.

Bivash Pandav

Peter Jackson

e a hunting preserve, the Keoladeo Ghana National Park hosts over 350 species rds. But it looks like the park's glory days are over. Its most famous visitor–the rian crane (below) no longer winters here, and the water politics is slowly draining, killing, this once-fecund wetland.

Joanna Van Gruisen

A marmot in the backdrop of the Tsokar Lake in Ladakh

The kiang, or the Tibetan wild
lives in alpine grasslands and
steppes of up to 5,000 me

Joanna Van Gruisen

er than 600 snow leopards now survive in India.

Vivek Sinha

lesser than 200 individuals, the hangul counts amongst world's rarest deer.

Bivash Pandav

In an ancient ritual called *arribada*, the olive ridley turtles arrive *enmasse* at their nesting site at the Gahirmatha beach in Orissa.

The Himalayan quail (above) was last seen in 1876, while the last record of the pink-headed duck (below) dates back to1936.

*Courtesy Bikram Grewal*

bills, such as the great hornbill, play a critical the survival and eration of forests attering seeds of the they feed on.

Abrar Ahmed

The king cobra is the la
venomous snake in the

What transpired over the next few days is difficult to describe, though the memories are clear as if it all happened last week. Small stuffy hotel rooms en route to Itanagar, shared by two adult human primates along with a full-sized, albeit dead, 15-kg non-human primate. Attempts to conceal our booty from the hotel staff, lest we get thrown out in the middle of the night. Even more desperate attempts to ignore the intensifying stench of the specimen. Getting our hands numb at the Sela pass, at an altitude of about 13,700 feet, collecting ice from a frozen river to prevent the specimen from rotting. Pleading with fish-sellers at fish markets en route for more ice. And, in the midst of all this, informing the relevant government authorities and getting permissions to transport and treat the specimen.

The two of us and our primate companion finally reached Itanagar Zoo, just in time, for a quick post-mortem by the zoo veterinarian, Jikom Panor. This was followed by the long, tedious process of treating the specimen.

Thus began our quest to unravel the mystery surrounding the evolutionary origins of the Arunachal macaque and the validity of its identity as a distinct species. We sought the help of our friend Uma Ramakrishnan and her colleagues at the National Centre for Biological Sciences, who were as excited about the possibility of uncovering the evolutionary secrets of this fascinating monkey as we were. Then began the laborious process of extracting the monkey DNA (the genetic blueprint of any species), amplifying it, sequencing it, and finally, comparing it with that of other closely related macaque species. We also included, in our analysis, the Assamese and Tibetan macaques of Eastern Himalayas and the bonnet and toque macaques of south India and Sri Lanka, respectively.

The results of all this work have surprised and fascinated us even more. To start with, our studies confirmed our belief that the Arunachal macaque was indeed a different species.

This result was only the beginning. Our measurements of the specimen showed that, in its anatomy, the Arunachal macaque was relatively closer to the Assamese and Tibetan macaques, species with which it shares its geographical distribution and ecological habitat. Yet, genetically, it was distinct from them, and, in fact, was surprisingly close to the bonnet macaque of south India, a monkey, which not only looks distinctly different but also occurs at least a thousand kilometres away!

We could also estimate that the Arunachal macaque, as we know it today, originated about half a million years ago, partly as a result of hybridisation between the ancestors of the modern-day Assamese macaque and the predecessors of the bonnet and the toque macaques. Finally, we now know that these species, including the bonnet and toque macaques of the southern latitudes, have all originated from a common ancestral macaque that inhabited the region of present-day Myanmar some four-and-a-half million years ago.

The Arunachal macaque has taught us much. Little had we anticipated that the much-celebrated discovery of the species was only the first step in a journey of a thousand miles, as aptly put by the Chinese philosopher Lao Tzu. The search for this enigmatic primate has truly been a most wonderful and rewarding experience for us. Of course, with each new research result, more intriguing questions seem to confront us rather than any easy answer. We will perhaps never know enough, but it is gratifying to see at least a few pieces of this infinite jigsaw puzzle of nature fall into place.

Charudutt Mishra and Anindya Sinha, 2008

# My Husband and Other Animals

*JANAKI LENIN*

*When you live in the Indian tropics, mofussil, whether it is in a mud-walled, thatch-roofed hut or the modern caveman's reinforced-concrete cave with fancy sliding windows, you share your life with creatures—myriads of creatures, large and small, innocuous, troublesome, always fascinating and occasionally, downright dangerous. And when your house is bordered by rice fields on one side and scrub jungle on the other, you've just upped the biodiversity odds by the power of ten. Janaki Lenin lives not far from the town of Chengalpattu, sixty kilometres south of Madras (now called 'Chennai'). Her house is located on a ten-acre tree farm (a euphemism for would-be farmers who've tried every other crop and failed), where, aside from occasional outbursts from temple loudspeakers, the dominant sounds here are birds (but no crows!). Night sounds are an array of owls, jackals (especially during the cool, rainy months) and every now and then, strange unidentified grunts from the forest. There are waterholes for creatures, fish keep the mosquito larva on their 'toes', and plenty of trees keep a diverse bird, lizard and squirrel population happy. Life is pretty busy on any farm and in her spare time former (she says) film maker, Janaki divides her time between writing on wildlife and getting her teeth into what she considers the conservation cause celebre: human/animal conflict mitigation. Her current project is a field and literature review of human/elephant conflict toward developing a jumbo mitigation action plan.*

'We've built a cave between the scrub jungle and the farmland and it's only natural to expect creatures to take advantage of it,' Rom warned when we first moved to our new home in the rural outskirts of Chennai. If he had meant furry mammals I would have been delighted but knowing him, he was definitely referring to creepy crawlies. While I nodded stoically, I was secretly questioning, 'Am I ready for this? Is it too late to bail out? Why didn't you tell me this before?' Within the first few months, we spotted a cobra in our backyard under the banyan tree, while our dog found a young Russell's viper crawling along the side of the house, metres away from the open kitchen door. Driving home late one night, we saw a common krait going past our gate. And within months, the local ladies cutting grass for their cattle found a couple of saw-scaled vipers. So, we had the 'Big Four' venomous snakes in the garden and I worried about playing host to one of them inside the house. Rom, however, was eagerly anticipating such an event, I suspected.

In the beginning, about nine years ago, the land was blistering hot and barren of trees. The scant shade was provided by the huge banyan and the hedge of palmyra trees. It was after all a rice field. We wasted no time planting trees around the house—the shade was sorely needed—and with daily watering, they shot up. At that time, we had hardly any furniture either, and every evening we unrolled our bedrolls on the floor. We had to shake out all the sheets just to make sure no creatures were hiding inside. Despite the exaggerated precaution, Rom shot out of bed one night in pain. A giant centipede had bitten him. The pain was so excruciating that he couldn't sleep the rest of the night. That was when we decided we needed to get above the floor and bought a cot.

In the adjacent scrub jungle, the largest wild mammals were jackals and bonnet macaques. We found porcupine quills and scats on the path created by the cows and goats. Optimistically, we planted peanuts the first year and lost some to the monkeys by day but most of it was lost at night. I assumed it was porcupines but our neighbours swore it was the jackals that were feasting on the peanuts and one early morning we saw them at it! After a few more such attempts we gave up trying to grow anything edible and stuck to trees.

One of the first interesting animals we saw was a ruddy mongoose. Until then, we had seen only the grey mongoose and were astounded to see this long reddish animal with upturned tail. The ruddy mongoose is almost as common in this area as the grey mongoose, and we have since seen several streaking across the road late in the evening, early in the morning and, on one occasion we saw a couple playing with the bonnet macaques on the hill. It was an overcast cool morning and we had a clear view of the hills in those early days. A troop of macaques was hanging out on the rocky hilltop waiting for the sun to come out. It was a peaceful scene until a pair of ruddy mongooses burst out of nowhere. With an easy familiarity, one of the young macaques pulled the tail of one of the mongooses, who turned around to chase the monkey. The other mongoose chased the first one and soon the monkeys and mongooses were gambolling on the hillside. Just as swiftly as it started, the game ended and the mongooses scurried off into the undergrowth.

It was approaching summer when the ubiquitous house geckos first moved in. This single event converted the house from a sterile enclosure into a 'home'. I just didn't have a clue to the number of creatures that were eventually going to claim our home as their own! One night, a little creature that I had never seen before, darted speedily across the room. It looked like a centipede with enormous thin legs. That was my introduction to the harmless scutigera (the house centipede). Common tree frogs began moving in as the heat built up. During the day they hid behind the framed pictures and at night they emerged to ambush the insects that hovered around the lights. Toads began to do the same in the garden.

At the height of summer, the frogs were everywhere (at one count, there were 289 in the house): in every crack, the tiniest of ledges, light fixtures, the toilet bowl and flush tank, behind cupboards. We check the inside of the washing machine before loading the laundry, because they are frequently inside (and sometimes even survive a whole wash cycle). At night they seek out the toilet bowl and kitchen sink to soak in before beginning the night's hunting. They spend a few minutes in the water and then wipe an oily lipid secretion all over their bodies with their hind legs. If you didn't chase them away before using the pot, with a flip of the flush, you would be treated to the rude shock of having a wet glob suddenly attach itself to your butt. At the fag end of the summer, the house resounds with their calls heralding the arrival of the rains. We try not to invite any guests then; the frog calls sound like a terribly flatulent person!

One of the hamlets close by is called 'Pulikudivanam' ('the woods where leopards live') and so, Rom christened our home 'Pambukudivanam' ('the woods where snakes live'). Our elderly neighbour, Thiruvenkatam, mentioned that we had unwittingly built our house on the spot where the last leopard was shot around these parts about thirty years ago. As we sat contemplating the sunsets over the last few years, we often wondered out loud whether a leopard would move in and debated whether it had a sporting chance of survival. Considering that the scrub jungle was more or less continuous up to Vandalur in the north and extends to the dry riverbed of Palar in the south (and perhaps beyond), wishing for a leopard here wasn't such a far-fetched fantasy. And sure enough, a few years later a male leopard was trapped at Vandalur.

About a year later, we noticed we had a new guest: a termite-hill gecko. It had staked out one of the kitchen cupboards as its territory. It was a very neat houseguest and always shat in one spot near the cupboard door making the cleaning very simple. One morning, when I opened the door to clean out the gecko's nightly offerings, there was a white round egg along with the little turds. Using a paintbrush I cleaned around it gently, taking care not to disturb the egg. A couple of days later, there was another egg until there was a collection of five. Months passed, nothing happened. The eggs grew discoloured and had to be cleaned out finally. I guess she had no male to fertilise the eggs.

Where frogs are, snakes can't be far behind. We've played host to a few in the last few years. The common bronze-back tree snake slides in through any of the upstairs windows from the overhanging banyan tree. One evening, we found one caught helplessly inside the wastebasket. That was odd as they are normally agile and acrobatic snakes. It was stuffed full of tree frogs, and was so satiated that it couldn't lever itself out! The night shift is taken over by the common wolf snake in its hunt for geckos. We've even had birds coming in to get the frogs. Drongos swoop in, grab a frog and sit on the window gruesomely bashing the frog into senselessness.

The floor of the upstairs is the domain of a large skink, a chunky, yellow-striped fellow. He lurks around through the day and retires under the cushion of the sofa for the night, just when we are about to relax in front of the TV. On rainy days, he can barely stir himself. It feels strange to pick up a pillow, like you'd turn over a rock in the garden, to find a nice fat skink sleeping underneath! Judging from the long healthy turds he leaves around, a lot of troublesome insects are getting chomped.

The creatures that turn our home into a real minefield are the scorpions. There are currently three different species residing at this address, but only one is dangerous – the red scorpion. They rule the windowsills, door and window hinges and perilously, the bookshelves as well. We never pull a book out by placing our fingers on top of the book's spine because that was where they hung out. A great book-thief deterrent!

Years passed before we noticed a new gecko on the prowl in the bedroom – the bark gecko. It made a meal of a few house geckos before staking out its large territory. Sometimes, when we returned home late and switched on the light, we caught a couple of these big geckoes engaged in mortal combat. They disengaged and ran across the floor in opposite directions with open wounds. If we hadn't unwittingly called off the battle, they would have almost certainly lost their tails and their skin would have been hanging in tatters. One evening, a false vampire bat began flitting through the house noiselessly. Watching him flap from room to room was like watching a Porsche being driven through congested city streets; he had to flap so slow that he could just barely be air-borne. He cleaned up all the geckos in the house in a couple of nights. Unfortunately, on one hot summer evening, I was cooling off under the fan when he got hit by the fast rotating blades and fell down stone dead. And now, the geckoes are back in profusion.

Quietly over the years, the house has become the summer home of a congregation of toads. Last summer, there were so many that we had to be very careful while walking around, for fear of stepping on one of them or their magnificently enormous scats. After a few days of cleaning up after them, I grew irritated; I wanted a normal house. So, I caught a whole bunch of them and moved them to the garden. They returned. I caught them all and moved them 250 metres away out of sight of the house. They were back that afternoon. They returned in 25 hours when I moved them 500 m away. That was it—it was an all-out battle of wits. By this time I had marked them with permanent marker so I could recognise them. I took them one km away across a road and into the scrub jungle. Maybe, that was too far away, or maybe they got the message that I didn't want them. Maybe, they all returned but stayed in the garden, I don't know. But the house was free of toads the rest of the summer and when the rains came we could hear their melodic metallic songs all around.

We are very careful where we put our hands and feet in the garden. Rat snakes have been our most common visitors over the years. We watched a pair of six-foot males fight for a couple of hours. Our big 30-foot-diameter well is ringed with several long nests of baya weaverbirds; one year we counted forty-three nests but it usually ranges in the 30s. One season, we watched a rat snake get into a nest and the whole thing, snake, nest and baby birds, fall into the well. The well was dry and the fall must have felt hard but the snake seemed to be alright. Comfortably grounded, he made short work of the baby birds.

We found a gravid slender coral snake under the banyan tree while digging a water pipeline, a Kollegal ground gecko in one of the dry watering pumps along with an incredibly fast pygmy shrew. This was great; we hadn't realised that these pretty geckoes, one of the world's smallest mammals, were found here.

Over the years, the price for living where we do was paid by our beloved dogs. We lost one to a cobra within a couple of years. That was the first time I had witnessed a snakebite incident and I was terrified of having venomous snakes around the house after that. We cleared all the overgrowth and made a policy decision that any venomous snakes in the garden would be removed to the forest hereafter. This year alone Rom has flipped seven Russell's vipers and a couple of cobras into the big bucket, and released them the next day, deep inside the scrub jungle.

At 10.30 p.m. on a late February night, 2005, Rom heard the distinctive sawing of a leopard. We went out into the garden, straining our ears for another chance to hear that call. The dogs had gone absolutely silent and Karadi, the male German Shepherd stood in the garden, bristling and growling. To Rom, that was confirmation that it was a leopard. For a few days after that, we listened intently for that particular sound but there were none. Perhaps, it was just passing through, Rom reasoned. 'Perhaps, it was just your imagination,' I thought to myself.

One cloudy afternoon, when I had a friend visiting me, the dogs found a young cobra. It had to be caught and moved into the forest. Rom was out so I had to play snake catcher for the first time. The dogs and friend were standing on one side while on the other was our pet pig's enclosure. I tried hooking the snake like I'd seen Rom do millions of times but the snake slipped off like spaghetti. Each time the snake slipped off the hook it crawled closer to Luppy, the pig. Luppy watched the cobra and grunted with interest. She would have a snack of the cobra if she got a chance! I felt clumsy and inept. Finally, the snake got tired and sat limply on the hook long enough for me to get it into a bucket. That's when I realised that I was shaking from the adrenalin rush and the fear that I was going to get bitten.

One night, our gardener came running to say there was a black and white banded snake in his house and it had crawled over him, as he was lying asleep. My mind kept saying 'krait'. Had a venomous snake finally found its way inside? What we found instead was a pretty snake appropriately called the bridal snake. While this was my first look at the species, Rom had last seen it thirty years ago in Guindy National Park, in the middle of Chennai city. A year later, on a nocturnal visit to the bathroom I saw another one on the windowsill and the little narrow-mouthed frogs were hurriedly seeking cover. That's the only indication we have of the bridal snake's diet. Since then we have found more than a dozen shed skins of this species draped on the rafters of our roof.

On several occasions over the years I have reared orphaned mongooses and toddy cats. One morning, the gardener brought a baby black-naped hare cupped in his hands. He said he saw the baby hare caught by a rat snake and it was screaming in terror. So, he had chased off the rat snake and rescued the hare. I scowled, 'But the rat snake has to eat too. Now, what do you want to do with the hare?' He may have been taken aback by my attitude and he then changed the story to—he was walking on the path and a rat snake had the hare in its mouth. Startled by his presence, the rat snake let go of the hare and disappeared. Whatever the story, we now had a really wee baby to look after. We took the hare back to the area and let it sit in a clump of grass and watched from a distance for several hours. There was no sign of mother nor was the baby stirring out of its hiding place. So, Jonah came to live with us.

Jonah hadn't been weaned yet. Priya, the vet, said that rabbit milk is very fatty and that regular cow's milk might have to be constituted with milk powder. So, Jonah lived on thick milk of a curd-like consistency. His 'form' was a basket with shredded newspaper during the day and at night he ran around inside the house. I provisioned him with fresh grass every evening so when he was ready for it, he could experiment.

A couple of months later, he was more than four times his original size and ready for the big world. We made a large cage for him and put him out every night on the edge where the forest meets our garden. After a few days of this, we opened the door and Jonah disappeared. I'd like to think he survived, but knowing what I now know about such rehabilitation efforts, I'm not so sure.

I felt bad about having to give away Jonah to the scrub but what really saddened me was losing my pet Karadi. Last month, in June, both of us were travelling when we heard the news that Karadi, our big male German Shepherd was missing. We thought he might have been stolen and sent instructions to paste posters offering a reward in all the nearby hamlets. A couple of days later, my parents, who live close by emailed saying they saw a large dog-like animal basking at sunset on the rocky outcrop of the hill and they wondered if it was a leopard. Soon after we arrived home, we hired a couple of Irula trackers and asked them to see what had happened to Karadi. We had already found the spot in the fence where he could have jumped over but it just didn't seem likely as the fence is lined on the inside with live cacti. The Irula studied the signs on the ground, found bits of fur caught in the cacti thorns and followed it into the forest. About 300 yards away from the fence, they found the remains of Karadi secreted amidst a miserably thorny thicket. Back-tracking, they found the spot in the garden where he had been killed. It had rained a couple of times and we could find no pugmarks but we were certain that it was a leopard.

We began making enquiries in the village: has anyone lost livestock? The answer was unanimously 'yes' but the villagers figured that it was a '*periya nari*' (translated literally 'big jackal'). One villager described the deep puncture wounds on the throat of the cow he had found dead in the forest. Undoubtedly a leopard's handiwork. Not wanting to cause panic, we were unsure about how to alert the villagers. Young 10-year boys often took goats into the forest and they could be in danger. Burdened by this moral obligation, we vacillated: should we or shouldn't we tell them what we thought. We prodded tentatively; could it have been a leopard (*sirutthai*). Several villagers categorically declared that 'those animals' were not here. We were puzzled by what '*periya nari*' could mean; wolf, hyena or jackal? This was a bit ridiculous, the idea that jackals would eat anything from peanuts to dogs! Finally, one villager said '*periya nari*' is '*sirutthai*' and it had spots. (According to Theodore Baskaran, the local name for tiger in the Annamalai area is '*periya nari*'.)

Most villagers said that they had begun losing livestock about a year ago, which puts it to the time when Rom had heard the leopard call. We have become more alert since then locking up the dogs at sunset, clearing the area around the house of all undergrowth and regularly scanning the boundary for eye-shine.

Having a leopard in one's front yard has irrevocably changed the atmosphere of the place. We pay a lot of attention to sounds and watch the hill with binoculars. Although I miss my dog very much, we probably would never have discovered the leopard's presence if Karadi had not been taken. We would have been dismissive of the villagers' stories of '*periya nari*' taking livestock and would have thought in our supercilious manner that the villagers really didn't know what they were talking about.

If the leopard knew how to lie low, moved from one village to the next without taking more than what the village could afford, didn't enter the village or take children, it could live in this marginal forest indefinitely. And it seems to me, that we are going to hear more and more of leopards staging a comeback in such marginal habitat. Whether it is going to be possible for man and these cats to co-exist remains to be seen.

# Saving the Indian Tiger: Where Do We Go from Here?

*K. Ullas Karanth*

*It can be safely said that Dr Ullas Karanth is responsible for infusing a strong dose of science into tiger conservation in India. He led the team that conducted a countrywide sample survey of tigers though the camera capture – recapture method which provided the first reliable estimates of tiger densities and emphasised the role of prey depletion in driving tiger declines. He also radio-collared tigers and leopards in Nagarhole National Park to understand their behaviour and biology. Though a scientist first, Karanth is no less a crusader. As director of Wildlife Conservation Society, a position he held for several years, he coordinated with government officials, foresters and NGOs to protect wild habitats. As a scientific advisor to several conservation groups, he played a key role in the voluntary relocation of villages from Bhadra Tiger Reserve and putting a stop to mining in Kudremukh National Park. In a grim scenario, he gives us a sense of optimism to tiger conservation, and shows us a path for the future.*

Walking down a typical Indian street, we can spot tigers everywhere: on panels of trucks, buses or rickshaws; on walls of rural schools, and, bill-boards touting movies or political rallies. The tiger stares back from signage promoting entities as varied as temples, holy men, auto-workshops or liquor bars. Centrality of the tiger is manifested through India's ancient religion, folklore and mythology, as well as its modern iconography of marketing around us.

Perhaps as a consequence, tiger conservation has been taken far more seriously in India than in any of the dozen other nations where this big cat hangs on grimly. This widespread concern, albeit lacking social depth, has led to massive media coverage of tiger issues and forty years of official conservation efforts. More recently, the concern got into lockstep with concerns about the country's international image, leading to the appointment of a prime ministerial Tiger Task Force (TTF) and substantially increased funding.

Some critics decry this concern as the preoccupation of an elitist 'tiger lobby'. I believe such criticism unjustified. Many other worthy causes, i.e. rights of women, *dalits* or *adivasis* in India are also promoted by the same 'social elite' that promotes wildlife conservation. If this does not make these other causes 'elitist', why should the conservation of tigers and other flagship species, whose broader goal is to protect natural landscapes, biodiversity and ecological security, be considered elitist? Therefore, conservationists have no reason to be shamed into feeling guilty about their commitment to the tiger's cause.

More practically, saving large, threatened forms of wildlife like tigers, elephants or rhinos, basically involves effectively protecting less than two percent of India's land area: making room for wild tigers is thus decidedly not some eco-fundamentalist call for embargo on all economic development or social empowerment across the entire Indian landscape.

However, there is so much bad news about tigers these days that conservationists appear to be giving up hope. Rapid economic growth, land-hunger of the poor, and thoughtless development projects are all pushing back tiger habitats. Even as pressure of poaching and habitat fragmentation mounts on tigers and their prey species, the guardians of India's forests—the Forest Departments in the states and the Ministry of Environment and Forests at the Centre—are drifting off-course, seduced by lucrative and headache-free distractions like 'eco-development', 'eco-tourism' and 'habitat management'.

The tiger's cause thus seems hopeless. Does it really? Jim Corbett had set the date for extinction of India's wild tigers as early as in the 1950s. Fifteen years ago, several leading conservationists had reset that clock and said wild tigers would be extinct by the year 2000. Although both deadlines have passed, about 1,500–2,000 wild tigers still survive in India.

When I was in school fifty years ago, tigers appeared to be far worse off than they are now. There were no effective laws to protect tigers from hunters, and habitats were being ripped apart by destructive forestry and development projects. In fact, there were official bounties for killing tigers and other predators. A villager I personally knew had shot twenty-seven tigers between 1948–65 to claim official rewards. He had shot them all around his village not far off from Nagarahole reserve in Karnataka. The social goal was to eliminate tigers through promotion of bounty hunting, sport hunting and even commercial safari-hunting well into the mid-1960s. Tougher wildlife conservation laws came only in 1970–80 period. Despite their recent unfortunate dilution under pressure from both the 'pro-people' and 'pro-industry' lobbies, these laws are still better than those of fifty years ago, and, than laws that prevail in most other tiger range countries. These laws need to be implemented effectively: something conservationists should be fighting for, instead of throwing up their hands in despair.

Fifty years ago, the Forest Department did not have a mandate to protect tigers, nor enough money for the task. Lone warriors like K.M. Chinnappa and Sanjoy Debroy struggled on with little more than their passion and commitment. Now, there is a clear mandate to protect tigers, and lots of money: egged on by conservationists the Prime Minister has earmarked six billion rupees in the current Five Year Plan for saving wild tigers. What conservationists need to do now is ensure proper use of these funds. A lot of this money is already being diverted for destructive habitat manipulations, eco-development, and such other follies. Focused use of these funds for tough protection on ground and generous voluntary relocation projects for local people who are locked in perpetual conflict with tigers, is something conservationists can now fight for.

Mere passion for the cause, however, is not enough: conservationists need to act in reasonable ways to make their passion work for tigers on ground. We have to act, but based on careful reasoning. Five decades ago, scientific methods of studying tigers were unknown and as a result, little knowledge of the ecology of the tiger was available. Since then, tiger research using modern scientific methods has generated substantial knowledge of tiger ecology. This know-how can help solve conservation problems and objectively evaluate successes and failures as we go along. How so?

The tiger's biology is literally rooted in its four dagger-like canine teeth. They permit the cat to kill a prey animal five times its own size with a single lethal bite. The tiger's diet consists of pure meat, and lots of it. It means that an average tiger needs

3,000 kilograms of live prey per year. A tigress raising cubs needs to kill 60–70 such prey animals per year. The 'success rate' of hunts is, however, one in ten, even for this efficient predator. Therefore, a single tiger requires a population of 500 prey animals to sustain it. Prey density thus determines how many tigers an area can hold.

Many tiger habitats of India are productive and hold lots of prey, if human hunters and livestock can be kept out. Alluvial grasslands and deciduous forests can hold up to 25–50 prey animals per sq km. As a result, a tigress can raise her cubs to dispersal age, within a small home range of 15–30 sq kms. Contrast this with the extremity of tiger habitats in the snow-bound Russian Taiga, where her home range would be 500 sq kms. Densities of adult tigers vary from a low of one tiger/100 sq km in Russia to 10–20 tigers per 100 sq kms in India's well-protected high quality habitats. This is good news for tiger conservation in India.

The scientific studies I conducted with support from Wildlife Conservation Society in eleven reserves across India have made this relationship clear. Alluvial grasslands like Kaziranga in Assam and deciduous forests like Nagarahole, Kanha and Bandipur in peninsular India, are packed with ungulates such as deer, pigs, nilgai, gaur and buffalo at high densities of 30–50 animals per sq km. Thus, tigers attain high densities of 12 to 18 animals per 100 sq kms (excluding small cubs). These productive habitats stand in stark contrast to inherently low-prey density habitats such as snow-bound Russian Taiga or Malaysian evergreen forests, where tigers can only occur at a tenth of these densities.

However, the same study showed that some other tiger reserves like Melghat and Bhadra, which could also potentially support 10–15 tigers per 100 sq km, hold only a third as many cats now, while other reserves like Namdapha are almost bereft of tigers because there simply is not enough meat on the hoof in these forests to support more wild tigers. When prey densities dip lower tigers cannot raise cubs and populations can persist only through periodic immigration from high-density source populations. This is the fate of most of India's tiger habitats now.

Productive source populations of tigers typically consist of several neighbouring tigresses that maintain distinct territories shared only with their dependent cubs, which they evict at two years of age to breed again. Adult male tigers compete amongst each other to gain mating opportunities with these resident tigresses. A male tiger's home range may, on an average, overlap three female territories. The female territories can be as small as 10 sq km or as large as 500 sq km, their size essentially being determined by prey abundance.

If there is enough prey, usually there are more adult tigers than there are available territories. These 'floaters' sneak about, looking for opportunities to evict a weak resident. Tiger society is fiercely competitive: violent fights, cub-killing by new territorial males, injuries suffered when hunting of prey, starvation and conflict with humans, all lead to high mortality rates. Only high reproduction can compensate these losses.

My long-term research in Nagarahole reserve shows that tiger is a resilient species with a high reproductive potential. A tigress starts breeding at the age of 3–4 years, and for the next 6–10 years produces 3 cubs once every 2 to 3 years. Achieving this reproductive potential depends on there being enough prey animals in the forest.

In this context, based on scientific inputs provided, the Tiger Task Force rightly recognised that a key challenge is to keep core tiger habitats 'inviolate' from incompatible human uses. The Task Force also recommended enhancing connectivity among tiger core populations through a variety of social tactics, not all of them realistic. Although the Task Force's restriction of such 'inviolate areas' to already notified Tiger Reserves, and limiting their total extent to just 37,000 sq kms, are clearly inadequate, the recognition of the need for inviolate critical tiger habitats has firm basis in science.

The Task Force also recognised that there are some unavoidable costs in terms of compensating humans who have to make room for wild tigers to maintain such critical tiger habitats. The challenge, therefore, is to develop different conservation models that work on the ground in specific local social contexts in a fair and effective manner, while meeting the tiger's ecological needs.

Currently, as found out in the recent Wildlife Institute of India survey, all of India's viable tiger populations are restricted to some areas in the Western Ghats, particularly Karnataka, parts of Central India in MP and Maharashtra, and a tattered arc of alluvial grasslands patches stretching from Uttaranchal to Assam. Land-cover maps show that these forests are all heavily fragmented. They are also set amidst regions of high human population density, faster economic growth and higher impacts of such growth. Yet, tigers are faring much better in these regions than elsewhere solely because of a few effectively protected tiger reserves embedded within a larger landscape matrix under multiple uses. Reserves such as Nagarahole–Bandipur, Kanha, Kaziranga and Corbett that support high prey densities serve as population sources where resident tigresses can maintain clusters of territories and successfully raise a surplus of cubs that disperse out into the surrounding population 'sinks'.

My long-term studies in Nagarahole show that although such healthy tiger populations suffer annual losses of 20 percent from natural mortalities and dispersal, these losses are more than made up by the high levels of reproduction. These productive source populations can take heavy losses without dipping down to unviable numbers. For example, a tiger population that I have studied for two decades in Nagarahole, had average annual losses of about 22 percent between 1991 and 2000, yet maintained high tiger density and recruitment, and, consequently an impressive long-term stability.

Thus, despite its many well-recognised problems, the 'exclusionary conservation model' centred on 'protected areas' has worked well to save tigers in many parts of India. On-ground anti-poaching patrols, village relocations and stoppage of all extractive forest uses, have staved off tiger extirpation in the above landscapes.

This status of affairs must be contrasted with another sobering aspect of the national tiger survey that has almost entirely escaped public attention. Over vast tracts of productive deciduous forest habitats that clothe northern Andhra Pradesh, Chhattisgarh, Orissa and Jharkhand, tiger populations have been decimated. The situation in the evergreen rainforests of North Eastern Hill states—Nagaland, Mizoram, Tripura, Arunachal, Meghalaya and Manipur—is even worse. Tigers are virtually gone from this region. The primary reason is that these forests have been emptied of tiger's principal prey—deer, pigs and wild cattle—by local traditions of massive hunting. These forests of India's predominantly tribal belt show up as beautiful swathes of green in remotely-sensed land-cover maps, thus accounting for most of our 'tiger habitats'. However, there simply is not enough food to maintain viable tiger populations under this beautiful canopy.

The superabundance of tigers earlier reported from reserves of this region, such as Orissa's Simlipal or Arunachal's Namdapha, merely reflected 'ghost tigers' generated by the now-discarded pugmark census method.

Why does the exclusionary conservation model that works for tigers elsewhere does not work in India's tribal belt, despite the latter's advantage of possessing more extensive stretches of forests, relatively lower human population densities and far fewer developmental pressures? There are several plausible reasons: political instability and armed insurgencies are widespread in this belt; social dominance and control over land vests largely with local communities. Strong traditional hunting skills, availability of newer weapons and market access to commercial wildlife trade are having a synergistic impact. The Forest Department is a largely passive bystander witnessing the resulting massive overkill and consumption of wildlife.

This leaves the field open for experimentation with inclusive tiger conservation models in which policing is de-emphasised. Although vociferously promoted for over a quarter century by international donor agencies and numerous votaries of community-based conservation jetting around the world, successful examples of such inclusive conservation models in India thus far appear to be restricted to little sacred groves that at best can hold smaller vertebrate species or endemic plants. Loud claims heard a few years ago about the tiger conservation successes under inclusive models at Sariska, Keoladevi and elsewhere are now muted, like the tiger's roar itself, at these locations.

There is not a single practical example—including the famous 'Periyar Eco-development model' which claims to have turned a handful of poachers into conservationists—where clear biological measurements are in place to show high tiger abundance and stable, viable tiger numbers, without strong law enforcement. So, let us leave the realm of speculation as to how tigers can be potentially saved under innovative inclusive models of conservation and return to the urgent issue of saving wild tigers here and now.

What do basic facts of tiger science mean for tiger conservation in India? In productive prey-rich habitats, a mere 1,000 sq kms of forests, a circle within a day's walk in any direction, can potentially hold 100–200 wild tigers. Even if 10–15 percent of these tigers are poached or disperse away annually, the population can still survive and be viable. Conservationists often forget that tigers are not like ancient fig trees: they replace themselves rapidly if there is enough food.

Various assessments show that 100,000–200,000 sq kms of potential tiger forests still survive in India. If conservationists can effectively engage on ground to protect patches of few thousand sq km at a time, many tiger populations can still be recovered. This will not be easy. Each recovery will be a slow, complex, painstaking mission extending over decades. There is no 'closure' in the business of tiger conservation.

Moreover, mere emotional commitment to the tiger won't help. Clear thinking and knowledge-based local advocacy must come into play at each tiger recovery site. While lobbying at the top political levels and pow-wows in high-power committees, conferences and task forces do matter, and, rallies and events in the big metros do keep the tiger buzz alive; timely local action at key tiger sites is the most critical element for success. And because time is slipping away, conservationists need to prioritise such action.

Fifty years ago, other than a handful of naturalists and hunters, no one else bothered about the fate of wild tigers or natural forests. Now, there is huge potential constituency for conservation within the rapidly growing rural and urban middle-class. If only conservationists can distract, say, five percent of the membership of this class, away from its current obsession with cricket, cinema and music videos, they can do a lot for tiger conservation. If those who preach ideologies of Maoism, Hindutva and such other causes can attract new recruits into their ranks from this middle-class, conservationists should also be able to do so. If tiger conservationists have the passion and commitment, India's wild tigers can still be saved.

Application of such science-based advocacy by local conservationists—where possible working in tandem with the few remaining committed forest officials—has resulted in tiger populations holding steady and even bouncing back at some of my study sites in Karnataka. Despite the bad news conservation struggles, at Nagarahole–Bandipur and Bhadra, I do catch one hundred tigers photographically in my camera traps each season. Tiger and prey numbers are rebounding in Bhadra. Local conservation leaders of a new generation, in this case, D. V. Girish in Bhadra, Pandira Muthanna in Nagarahole and others like them, are making a difference for tigers on the ground. While these are, indeed, extraordinary individuals, I am sure many others like them are hidden undiscovered in our vast country. Such conservation warriors need to be identified locally, energised and supported over long term. I think therein lies the primary conservation challenge in sustaining wild tigers into the next century and beyond.

Synthesised from:
'Recovering India's Wild Tigers', *The Hindu* Survey of the Environment, 2008; and 'Saving the Indian Tiger' *Sanctuary Asia,* June 2008

# India's Vanishing Birds

*BIKRAM GREWAL*

*Bikram Grewal is the 'bad boy' of Indian ornithology, though there lurks the doubt that this image has been carefully cultivated. Bikram's interest in birds dates back to his student days, when he started out as a closet birdwatcher (because, he says, it was not quite the thing to do in a boy's boarding school). He grew up to be the strongest voice on bird protection in India and has authored various books on Indian birds and wildlife. He is a publisher by profession, loves to travel, and lives the dream that he will rediscover the now-extinct Mountain Quail. Bikram believes that birds and their habitats are poorly defended by established conservation organisations in India. In this piece, he draws attention to the critically endangered birds of the subcontinent and those that have gone over the brink. It's not all bad news though, as the author tells us happy stories of birds 'back from the dead', some rediscovered after they were thought to be extinct for over a century.*

One of the most significant and exciting achievements of Indian ornithology, in recent years, was the rediscovery of the Jerdon's Courser in 1986. The last authentic record, by Howard Campbell, was in 1900. First recorded by Capt. Surgeon T.C. Jerdon, an Indian Army Medical Officer, in 1848, it was subsequently reported by Blanford in 1867 and 1871. Always a rare bird, these limited sightings were restricted to a few river valleys in Andhra Pradesh. Despite surveys by reputed ornithologists like Salim Ali and Hugh Whistler, the bird remained unseen. In January of 1986, a young scientist, Bharat Bushan, from the Bombay Natural History Society, finally rediscovered the bird, which was found to be mostly nocturnal. Jubilation engulfed the entire birding fraternity. However, its current status remains as fragile as ever. A similar joyful story involves the Forest Spotted Owlet, one of India's most elusive birds. After its last-confirmed sighting in 1884, there were several attempts to re-locate this bird and finally, in 1997, a team including Ben King and Pam Rasmussen came upon one in the Dhule region of Maharashtra.

Till recently, there existed only one confirmed specimen in the world of the Large-billed Warbler collected by the legendry A.O. Hume at Rampur Bushair on the River Sutlej in Himachal, in November 1867. This bird was not found for the next 139 years, till Philip Round mist-netted a live bird in Thailand in 2006. Sumit Sen and his team found and photographed this elusive bird in Narendrapur near Kolkata the next year. I was lucky to see a pair at the same place. It has never been seen again in India! There are, however, some unsubstantiated reports from the Kanha area in Madhya Pradesh.

Another bird species that has been presumed extinct for several decades is the pink-headed duck. It was always thinly distributed through the wetlands, swamps and wilderness areas that formed around the river systems of the vast plains of Bengal and what is now Bangladesh. The reed-beds along the rivers have now long since been cleared by the burgeoning human population and the isolated enclosed waters have disappeared. Little is known about this duck and only a handful of skins remain in museum collections. It was last reliably seen in 1936, though it is possible that a few survived as late as the 1940s in private collections in England. A few claimed sightings in recent years have not been accepted. A duck that might meet a similar fate in India is the White-winged Wood Duck. This forest duck is in danger of extinction, largely because it has a very small and fragmented population, which is undergoing a very rapid and continuing decline as a result of deforestation, wetland drainage and hunting. Nameri, in Assam, is about the only place it can be reliably found, though I drew a blank on a recent trip there. Only about four hundred survive in India, and an equal number is distributed in the neighbouring countries in South-east Asia. Other ducks under threat and suffering from the loss of suitable habitat and hunting include the Andaman Teal, the Fulvous Whistling Duck, the Comb Duck and the Cotton Pygmy Goose.

Little is known about the Himalayan Quail, which was first reported in 1846, from a private collection in England, and last seen in 1876. Always a difficult bird to flush and the few specimens that were found are from the Mussourie and Nainital areas of Uttarakhand. Several expeditions to find the bird have returned empty handed.

But there have been some other wonderful stories as well and one concerns the Mishmi (Rusty-throated) Wren Babbler, which was known from one dead female specimen collected by Dillon Ripley and Salim Ali from the Mishmi Hills area of Arunachal Pradesh in 1947. No individual was seen again till Julian Donahue and Ben King managed to lure one out in November 2004. Since then, it has been established as being locally common. But perhaps, the happiest story of all is the discovery of a completely new species, The *Bugun liochicla*, which was discovered during the Eaglenest Biodiversity Project initiated by Ramana Athreya in partnership with one Mr Indi Glow of the Bugun tribe, who live on the periphery of Eaglenest Sanctuary in Arunachal Pradesh. A series of observations in 2005 and 2006 confirmed its taxonomic status as a species new to science and it was formally announced to the world on 12 September 2006.

This thrilling discovery hides a very serious trend in the world of Indian conservation, as birds are treated as second-class citizens and (along with butterflies, insects, fish and snakes) are a major victim of 'mega-fauna hegemony', which in simple words means that most of the money spent goes to the tiger, at the cost of lesser denizens. The fact that there are under six hundred Great Indian Bustards left in the world does not seem to concern the powers that be. Why should this large bird be any less important than the tiger? The fate of its lesser cousins, the Bengal and Lesser Florican, is even more dismal and the day of their extinction may not be far away. Loss of habitat, particularly the grasslands, is a major cause of their decline. Under pressure from the ever-growing population, large tracts of land are being converted into agricultural land. It is not only the large birds that are being threatened by this mad rush for cultivable land. Smaller game birds like francolins, partridges and quails are losing their breeding territories. Smaller grassland birds like bushchats and stonechats too are declining. Birds once common are also causing concern. There are alarming reports that the numbers of the House Sparrow are declining rapidly, at least in the urban areas, due to the concretisation of our cities and towns.

About eight percent of India's birds are under extreme threat. The plight of the vulture is well documented. The offending drug, Diclofenac, has finally been officially banned, but is still in surreptitious use. This, along with the shortage of suitable tall trees to breed and the changing pattern of milk production resulting in the reduction of dead cows to feed on, may mean that we lose them in our lifetime. The loss of tall trees has also affected the breeding of birds like all the hornbills, the Greater and Lesser Adjutants and the Black-necked Stork. The draining or drying up of wetlands has meant that birds like the already endangered Swamp Francolin are losing their habitat. Political games often result in man-made disasters, as was highlighted in the recent case of Bharatpur, India's showcase wetland. Water was denied to it and instead, diverted into the fields in order to garner popular political support. Already in the public eye, because its most famous visitor the Siberian Crane stopped coming from 2002, this Ramsar Site and World Heritage Site is being destroyed.

What do we do to prevent and arrest this decline of our avian wildlife? Hunting is a major problem and the illegal netting of game birds for food and the trapping of pheasants for the pet trade continues unabated. The entire tribal belt in the north-east believes that hunting is their birthright. Another passing concern is about the continuing preservation of their habitat. But our chosen path is a destructive one. A series of ill-planned development projects has destroyed the entire Teesta Valley in Sikkim. Now, the last of our pristine forests in Arunachal Pradesh will drown under a series of dams. All across India habitats are being degraded and destroyed. If this continues, there may come a time when the air is bereft of birdsong.

# Corbett—Eternal: In the Shadow of Jim's Past

*Tom Alter*

*Most of us know Tom Alter as the actor who has portrayed a gamut of roles in television, films and theatre. He has essayed characters ranging from the quintessential sahib to the heartless villain, the gentle father to the erudite scholar, from the poet Ghalib to the freedom fighter Maulana Azad. His knowledge of and proficiency in Urdu, Hindi, English and the Indian culture make him one of the most versatile of Thespians in the country. Awarded the Padma Shri in 2008, Alter has worked with stalwarts such as Satyajit Ray and Ismail Merchant. Alter is as versatile a writer as he is an actor, having authored three books (and promises he is penning his fourth). He has another hidden passion – wildlife; and the Corbett Tiger Reserve—a legacy of the famous hunter-conservationist, Jim Corbett—is his first love. He writes of his early experiences in this beautiful land of trumpet and roar, and of a love that only grew in years with an impressionistic sensitivity.*

Early, early morning, winter, cold, intimate, I quietly open the door of the old Sarapduli forest bungalow. As the wooden door creaks open, I hear the river over the rocks, I hear the wind through the almost dark; I hear my heart.

Clad in my school tracksuit, a gift from an older woman who was the school's greatest runner and my secret heartthrob, I am away down the track, which leads to the main road.

The track is damp with dew, and the trees still sleep in the growing light. I pass the quarters where the forest guards and the *chowkidar* live; I pass the old gate; I pass Jim Corbett, smoking his *bidi* and sipping his tea, nodding in approval of my run.

I turn right, headed towards Dhikala, 13 km away.

I was 17, in my final year at school; my final winter vacation; my final visit to the Corbett Park; a winter tradition that my parents started so many years earlier.

I am still 17; I am still running from Sarapduli to Dhikala on an early, early winter's morning.

The gravel and grass underfoot is fresh, and yet so familiar.
Each bend, each sudden stretch of open glade – favourite lines of poetry.
Chital, a sudden sambar, birds of so many kinds.
A wild pig; thankfully, at a distance.
A tiny *kakar*, darting down the road, and then disappearing. . . .
The gathering light; the Ramganga singing in the distance.

The first rush of fatigue, and the steady return of rhythm.
Elephants—a good herd—far down the road.

Six kilometres to go; the light in shadowed streaks now across the road, through the trees; my breath; part of the forest now, part of the wild.

Corbett high in a *machaan*; still smoking; rifle eased over bent knee, eyes searching for any sign, any hint of eager danger. I reach the Dhikala gate, but do not enter, everywhere is the morning, everywhere the scent of the day.

The return run is easy and joyful, and my mother is waiting for me, hot cup of tea in hand. What is it about Jim Corbett, among all the *shikaris* of the British Raj that makes him so special? And the park, named after him, the ultimate destination?

Is it simply because he wrote about his exploits, his hunting success? Is it simply because he was the last great *shikari*, before Independence and the 'permit Raj' ended an era forever?

Why do I remember a morning's run so vividly after 40 years?

Was it simply because I was running through Corbett Park?

Questions, which truly need no answers, and yet must be answered.

Over the past year, I have been privileged, have been thrilled, to be part of a revival of the Corbett legend, which culminated in Jim being the hero of the Uttarakhand float at the Republic Day Parade on 26 January 2007. I was shooting a film deep in the Andamans, and yet through phone calls and messages from very excited friends, I received the news that Jim was, indeed, the hero of Uttarakhand. My friends were watching the parade on television, and then, suddenly, there was Jim atop the float. And they immediately tried to get in touch with me, to share the joy.

An Englishman, atop the float of a new state, in a parade, which is the ultimate display of patriotism and national power and pride, which our country, once a year, indulges in.

> Jim would have had a smile on his lips, tears in his eyes, and as usual, little to say.
>
> But in his heart, there would be tremendous joy and pride.
>
> Jim Corbett loved India; all you have to do is read his book, *My India;* each page, each story, each memory tells of a man for whom India was not only home, but the very source of his inspiration—
>
> And the people of Kumaon, the part of India that was Corbett's home, still remember him as 'Carpet-*sahib*'. He cared for and loved his people, his land, his forest with a committed passion that created the legacy, the burden, the challenge, which today's environmentalists, today's naturalists, today's conservationists, today's wildlife lovers learn from, and carry on from.
>
> Read the introduction of *My India*, and you will sense the wisdom and love of Corbett for Kumaon and her people; his love for the wildlife, for the jungle; his love for life, and all its manifold mysteries.

Of course, another reason why we love Jim and his writings so much is that he is an amazing writer, an amazing storyteller. Read, or re-read *Jungle Lore;* see the humour of Jim, the tongue-in-cheek zest of the man as he talks about his childhood, about his early experiences in the forest, or with fellow-human beings—men and women.

Read about his time in the railways, or in the Second World War, teaching jungle-knowledge to the soldiers headed into Burma.

Read about his time behind the camera – the deeper challenge of that technical marvel over his beloved rifle.

And then, return to his *shikar* stories, and you will find there, as he hunts, all the passion and care, which made him, in his later years, the greatest protector of both tiger and leopard.

Jim grew up in a small village called Kaladhungi, at the base of the first great rise of the Himalayas, leading up to Nainital, where Jim's father and brother, and Jim himself, worked.

*Jungle Lore*, my favourite Corbett book, begins from Kaladhungi.

Today, Jim's old bungalow is a museum, complete with bookshop and souvenir store and old photographs and Corbett memorabilia, to sit on the verandah and sip tea, as the evening gathers in the trees where Corbett actually saw the infamous *churail* is to wallow gently in the Corbett myth.

Behind the bungalow are forty acres of land, which once belonged to Corbett, and which he bequeathed to the villagers when he left India so suddenly in 1947. Today, that land, that village called Chhoti Haldwani, is home to many children whose grandparents would have known Corbett, hunted with Corbett, laughed and joked with Corbett, shared tea and cigarettes.

And twice last year, in memory of Corbett's birth and death, those children joined together at the village *chaupal*; the first time to read from *Jungle Lore*, in Hindi translation, and sing and dance in Corbett's honour; the second time, to put on a play, again in Hindi, of Corbett's life, inspired by his books.

There was Corbett—all four feet of him—in '*sola Topî* ' and *khakhi dress*—moustache hanging desperately onto young lips, there were all the characters from his stories; there was Maggie, his beloved sister, in white skirt; such a delight it was.

And the children of Chhoti Haldwani, with each word, each song, each sense; learning of their legacy—the legacy of Jim Corbett.

With the Boar river bridge, from where *Jungle Lore* begins, only a ten-minute walk away.

Things have changed, of course.

Today, in Corbett Park, I would not be allowed to run from Sarapduli to Dhikala, for reasons of my own safety, and the privacy and safety of the animals. I would not be allowed to walk, alone, fishing along the way, from Sarapduli to Gairal.

There are many, many more people visiting the park now. People of all types, all passions.

Hence, the new rules; the new regulations. And yet, at the end of 2006, when I visited the park after a gap of eighteen years, with family and friends for whom the park was equally beloved, we were not disappointed.

On the grasslands near Dhikala, we sighted a tiger so close to us, that we could not breathe.

My friend and I were standing in the back of the open jeep, my favourite teacher from school in the front. Suddenly, I spotted the tiger, only five metres away to my left. He appeared a mirage; but he was real, and staring straight at me.

I whispered to the driver to stop the jeep.

And as we reversed the jeep towards the tiger, all four of us, the driver included, knew the strength and power and dignity and grace of the animal.

The animal Corbett had hunted and loved so much.

We watched the tiger for about thirty seconds; he was staring straight into my eyes.

Nothing separated us but thin air; and his compassion.

And that evening, in the lovely amphitheatre at Dhikala, I read, in a fine Hindi translation, to the gathered tourists and their children, of Corbett. I read the chapter from *My India,* titled, 'Pre-Red Tape Day'.

Read it; there is no mention of *shikar*, or even wildlife, but it tells of the people of Kumaon, and their beauty, and their problems, and the problems of India, and the beauty of India.

My favourite Corbett story?

From memory, two incidents come back.

The first one, when he had just collected some rare bird-eggs, and was holding them in his left hand, and suddenly a leopard jumps on him from atop a high rock, and he swivels around to fire, one-handed, and slays the leopard – and keeps the eggs intact.

The other, when he is sitting up all night in a village hut, expecting the man-eating leopard to appear at any minute, and he suddenly feels feline whiskers on his neck. Frozen with fear, he spends the night without moving, almost without breathing; and then, with dawn's light, finds the village cat asleep at his feet.

And complete stories? My favourite is *The Man-eating Leopard of Rudraprayag* – for sheer story-telling, attention to detail, human frailties, the leopard's magic, fatigue, despair, and final triumph. It is a story of not only *shikar*, but of the relationship which animals and humans share with each other, and their jungle.

By the time you finish the book, the Rudraprayag area has become battleground, playground, and home. You can actually feel the grass and rock underfoot, hear the sounds of the villages, and above all, sense the terror and truth of the leopard, and Corbett's very human determination to first understand the leopard, and then to conquer it. An example:

> *. . . but my luck was out; for the night had hardly fallen when there was a flash of lightning, followed by distant thunder, and in a few minutes the sky was heavily overcast. Just as the first big drops of a deluge began to fall, I heard a stone roll into the ravine, and [a] minute later the loose straw on the ground below me was being scratched up. The leopard had arrived, and while I sat in torrential rain with the icy-cold wind whistling through my wet clothes, he lay dry and snug in the straw below. The storm was one of the worst I have ever experienced, and while it was at its height, I saw a lantern being carried towards the village, and marvelled at the courage of the man who carried it. It was not until some hours later that I learnt that the man who so gallantly braved both the leopard and the storm,*

*had done a forced march for over 30 miles from Pauri to bring me the electric night-shooting light the government had promised me; the arrival of this light three short hours earlier might . . . but regrets are vain, and who can say that the fourteen people who died later would have had a longer span of life if the leopard had not buried his teeth in their throats? And again, even if the light had arrived in time there is no certainty that I should have killed the leopard that night.*

The uncertainty of both life and death—and Corbett wrote this story many, many years later, sitting at 'Tiger Tops' in Kenya; just as Kipling wrote *The Jungle Book* so many years after leaving India, sitting in Vermont, in a house he named 'Naulakha'.

The jungles of India, and the rulers of those jungles, both human and animal—that fragile relationship will never end, because, in honour of Corbett, we must never allow it to end.

Our family visited Corbett Park roughly eight times in the 1960s and early 1970s. We stayed at Boxar (now under water, but the setting of Corbett's story on 'red-tape' that I mentioned earlier), Gairal and Sarapduli.

And it was my father, now fishing the waters of heaven, who was the inspiration behind our trips to Corbett. My mother, of course, did all the preparations and packing and planning of meals and clothes; but it was my father, who, with trembling fingers, taught us how to tie on the swivel, and look for the pools just behind the rocks at the head of the rapids.

On one of my last visits to Corbett with my father in the early 1970s, I wrote a poem for him, and for Corbett; both the park and the man:

*We went, my father and I,*
*down into the pines along the ridge,*
*down into the reeds along the pond,*
*down into the rocks along the river—*
*he smiled at me, quickly,*

*and then fell asleep in the shade—*
*I dreamed on,*
*and my dreams covered great peaks and great valleys,*
*moments of love and passion,*
*and the quick twist of muscle, tight under the skin—*
*I came from him, all of me—*
*he is my father—*
*he awoke,*
*and together we forded the river,*
*just above the rapids,*
*where the crossing is best—*

*The Corbett Inheritance* by Brijendra Singh,
Bittu Sahgal and Bikram Grewal,
Sanctuary Asia, 2007

# New Year at Gopalsamibetta

*S. Theodore Baskaran*

*S. Theodore Baskaran, is ruled by two vastly divergent passions—cinema and wildlife. Though one is slightly unclear how his interest in the former was born, he cut his teeth in the natural world very early in life. Growing up in the village of Dharapuram—the author says that 'most of their (he and his siblings) waking days were spent in the open. He explored the countryside, rescued and brought up a jungle cat and other assorted animals, fished with a bamboo stick – and this early association nurtured in him a love for nature. He describes his relationship with wildlife as intuitive . . . and it is this bonding that is evident in his writing. Baskaran is a film historian and has been given the Swarnakamal Award by the President of India. He was written extensively in newspapers and magazines, and also authored* The Dance of the Sarus. *In this essay, the wandering naturalist travels to Gopalsamibetta, and through the easy crafting of words takes us to the Bandipur Tiger Reserve in Karnataka, and the hills that encircle this beauteous forest.*

In the north-eastern periphery of Bandipur National Park stretches a range of hills called Gopalsamibetta (1,468 m) that takes its name from the temple on top. It was to this place we headed on the 31st of December 2003, keeping up with the family tradition of ushering in the New Year in a forest. It was late afternoon when we arrived there, having left Mysore after a leisurely breakfast.

This hill temple, dedicated to Lord Vishnu, has few devotees visiting. The brick and mortar shed meant for the temple chariot is now occupied by a posse of police of the Special Task Force. It was formed to catch Veerappan, the bandit, who had been operating in the forests of Bandipur and surrounding areas for more than ten years.* They had set up a radio station in the shed. A wall of huge granite boulders had once surrounded the temple. Beyond the temple, remnant of massive battlements could be seen. There is a look-out post with a clear view of the Mysore–Ooty highway snaking across the dry plains.

What is intriguing is that across the next hill also runs a wall of immense proportions with an opening in one end. Against whom or what was this wall built? When? Later, thumbing through the *Mysore Gazetteer* (1897) at the Mythic society library in Bangalore, I was to learn that this fort was known as Bettekotta (hill fort) and was built by a poligar Somanna Danayaka, in the later part of the eighteenth century. He is one of the nine Danayaka brothers of tradition. (Poligars, anglicised version of

---

* India's 'most wanted' forest brigand, Veerappan, had eluded the law for years and was finally killed in October 2004.

the Tamil term *Palayakarar*, were the vassals of the Nayaks of Madurai. Some of them offered resistance to the East India Company but were quickly put down.) Quite a few forts in this area are attributed to these brothers. One such was submerged when the dam across the river Bhavani near Sathyamangalam was built and a huge reservoir came into being.

Close to the temple, on the shoulder of the hill is a forest rest house built in 1933, credited with the barest necessities. No electricity. Like the other colonial-era rest houses, this one also commands a stunning view of a wide valley on the left and the plains of Gundelpet on the right. A trench, to keep the elephants off, encircles it. Inside the rest house, a large photograph of a hunting party with a slain tiger in the foreground adorns the wall. Closer examination reveals the slayer in the centre of the group as none other than Lord Irwin, Viceroy of British India. The Maharajas of Mysore and Bikaner flank him dutifully. A tiger hunt was something Indian kings organised to honour their imperial guests, a colonial equivalent of a banquet.

After handing over rice and dal for our supper, we set out on the bridle path that led into the grassland on the other slope. It was mountains and forests all around. The shrill drone of cicadas that pervaded the jungle rose up to a crescendo, stopped abruptly, only to begin tentatively again a few seconds later. The caretaker of the rest house insisted on accompanying us, with his double-barrelled breach-loader slung rakishly across his shoulders. I did not go into the question of how he was going to protect us with a shotgun from elephants, the evidences of whose presence was all around in the form of heaps of dung.

An outcrop of bare rocks jutting out of the hill, hewn into different shapes by eons of wind and rain, appeared like a sculpture gallery of Henry Moore. As you got closer, the multi-coloured lichen sticking to the rock could be seen. A brown rock thrush perched on one of the rocks, deftly balancing itself against the wind. On a dead tree stump, clung a rock lizard in an amazing display of camouflage. Even as you were looking at it seemed to disappear and reappear.

The folds of the valley were clothed in dense forest. You could see the bottom of the fold was like a green ribbon, indicating the presence of a stream. There were many such streams in these parts and it is here that river Kabana originates. Though most of them were dry now, Ginger lily plants growing at the edge of the forest indicated that the valley had been very wet. Orchids abounded on the trees. We could hear the clear belling of a Sambar from inside the patch of forest in the valley. It is typical Sambar country and home for this deer in vast numbers. Next morning, we would spot nearly fifteen of them. This large deer is a favoured prey for tiger.

The ranges of the hills seem to extend endlessly. The slanting rays of the sun accentuated the folds and valleys. The grasslands took on a golden hue as the sun, like a sliver of fire, began sliding behind the ranges. The evening turned cold rapidly. A tenacious lone black-winged kite was hovering over the grassland even as darkness engulfed the hills. A few stars began appearing tentatively and soon the clear moonless sky was filled with myriad stars. The Milky Way could be seen distinctly. We hurried back to the rest house. After an early dinner of rice and a fried dal of sorts, we snuggled inside our sleeping bags. An occasional belling of Sambar floated from the valley intensifying the silence of the night.

The crowing of Jungle fowl announced a glorious morning. This magnificent pheasant, nearly shot out of existence a few decades ago for the pot and more for its neck feathers used as fly lure in fly-fishing, is now secure in these sanctuaries. The mist was lifting and the morning sun was pouring gold over the landscape. We walked along the ridge of the hill, following a bridle path that cut through the grassland. A Pale harrier, a migrant raptor, had already started scanning the grassland flying low. A common sergeant butterfly briefly landed on a clump of grass before setting off to an unknown destination.

We could spot two gaurs, in different parts of the hill. Their massive body glistened in the morning sun as they grazed contently. When the sun rose a little higher and grew warm, the gaurs disappeared into the forest. It is in the Western Ghats that these bovines attain their maximum proportions. Though these animals are susceptible to diseases like anthrax and rinderpest, brought in by domestic cattle and the calves often fall prey to tigers for now their population is stable. You get to see them easily in all the sanctuaries in the Western Ghats.

There were signs of the presence of other mammals. We could identify droppings of porcupine and hare all over. There were three lumps of tiger scat, in different stages of decomposition. The oldest was a just tight lump of Sambar hair and bones. Scat analysis is a handy tool for wildlife biologists. Learning of the big cat's presence there lent an aura to the place. Bandipur National Park was declared a Project Tiger area when the project was launched in 1973.

Driving back to Bangalore, we stopped at a wayside dhaba and as we waited for tea, we tallied our bird list. We had sighted seventy-six birds. Though it was poor compared to the 125 of last New Year at Nagerhole, the consolation for me was that it included two lifers (birds you sight for the first time in your life): grey nightjar and a black redstart, a tiny flycatcher that breeds in the Himalayas and winters in the Western Ghats.

Courtesy: *The Hindu Sunday Magazine,* 15 June 2003

# Barefoot among the Turtles

*SHEKAR DATTATRI*

*Shekar Dattatri is a wildlife and conservation filmmaker based in Chennai, whose lifelong fascination for nature began at the age of ten, when he first read a book by Gerald Durrell. During the last twenty years, he has produced many award-winning documentaries that have been aired around the world on channels such as Discovery and National Geographic. Having moved away from television documentaries, he now focuses his attention on producing conservation films in collaboration with scientists and NGOs in India. Some of these films, like 'Mindless Mining – The Tragedy of Kudremukh', have been instrumental in bringing about positive change. The following piece is his account of the incredible natural phenomenon of mass nesting of the olive ridley turtles in Orissa. It is also an eyewitness account of the plight of the ridleys, tens of thousands of which have died in the last decade due to callous fishing practices and habitat destruction.*

*They emerged from the sea in thousands, slick shells glistening in the moonlight; the beach was soon covered with prehistoric shapes, and a strange drumming resounded through the air. Virtually within the blink of an eye, I seemed to have been transported back in time, to a period when dinosaurs ruled the earth.*

*In half a lifetime of roaming the Indian wilderness, I've had my share of adventure and unique experiences; but for sheer spectacle and atmosphere, nothing can compare with that night, over twenty-five years ago, when I witnessed my first 'arribada' – the mass nesting of olive ridley sea-turtles on a moonlit beach.*

A freelance nature photographer at the time, I had been commissioned by *Sanctuary* magazine to document this awesome event. Loading my backpack with camera equipment, a few clothes and a torch, I caught the Coromandel Express from Chennai on the first leg of my journey towards Gahirmatha Beach in Orissa, one of the few places in the world where one could witness this natural extravaganza. The train journey was uneventful and soporific but when I awoke early the next morning to get off at my station, there was a nasty surprise in store: someone had pinched my boots! The shops wouldn't open for a few hours and I still had a long way to go. Feeling somewhat odd in my bare feet, I caught a bus to the river port of Chandbali, my entry point to the Bhitarkanika wildlife sanctuary.

Leaving town, the bus bounced enthusiastically along pot-holed roads, and after a couple of bone-jarring hours we ground to a halt next to a jetty on the banks of the Baitarani River. After a quick meal at a ramshackle eatery, I hired a boat for the next stage of my adventure.

The diesel-engine boat navigated slowly through creeks flanked with verdant mangrove vegetation. Here and there, small herds of spotted deer peered at us from little glades, while egrets patrolled the water's edge, gazing intently into the murky depths for a meal. Dazzling black-capped kingfishers flitted past, their feathers iridescent in the sunlight. A six-foot long, black and yellow, water monitor-lizard prowled through the mangrove roots, unmindful of our noisy passage. And, as we turned a bend in the creek, a magnificent 15-foot-long saltwater crocodile lay basking on the bank, its mouth open to reveal fearsome teeth. As the boat drew closer, the giant reptile slid on its belly and slipped into the water with scarcely a ripple.

The winter sun was crisp but mild, and it was exceedingly pleasant to be out on the deck of the boat. There was always something to catch the eye in the mangroves. Occasionally, we passed local fishermen in small canoes, setting their fishing nets across creeks. Time passed slowly and it was several hours before we entered a broad expanse of backwater. The driver switched off the engine and let the boat drift in silence until it came to a halt. This was as far as he could take me.

After hours of being forced to listen to the noise of the engine, the silence that followed was sheer bliss. Now, the only sounds were of water lapping against the hull and the chirping and squawking of hundreds of waders and sea birds. The sun had set a few minutes ago in a blaze of colour and twilight was upon us. It was time for me to leave the boat and set off on the last leg of my journey on foot. Since the tide was out, the boat could not get close to the shore. So, I rolled up my pants and climbed out into the waist-deep water. At another time I might have worried about lurking crocodiles, but at that moment I was only focused on reaching the shore a hundred metres away. For just beyond it lay the nesting beach and the Bay of Bengal.

I waded through the water and emerged onto a mud flat. Now, only fifty metres remained to the shore, but it turned out to be the toughest fifty metres I've crossed in my life. The black mangrove mud was thick and gooey and, with every step I sank deeper into it. What was amusing at first soon turned alarming, for, within just a few paces, I was mired up to my waist, and couldn't move an inch! To make matters worse, the boat had turned around and was heading back, leaving me helplessly marooned. Luckily, the boat driver had seen my predicament, and returned some minutes later with a tiny, country fisherman's canoe in tow. The local fisherman had been fishing in a nearby creek and had been about to head home. Grinning good naturedly, he pushed his light wooden dugout on to the mud flat, and I managed to extricate myself from the quagmire by clinging on to the canoe and sliding it towards the shore. By the time I set foot on solid ground I was caked in thick mud, exhausted and uncomfortable, but exhilarated. Thirty-six hours after I had left home, I had finally reached Gahirmatha, one of the most remote and wild beaches in all of India.

Twilight soon turned to darkness and the star-studded sky was a sight to behold. I washed myself as thoroughly as possible in the sea and emerged feeling rejuvenated. A strong, cold wind began to whip the sand, which stung my bare legs as I began my final trek at a brisk pace towards the field camp of Chandrasekhar Kar, a sea turtle biologist who was studying the olive ridley arribadas.

I had walked only a kilometre or two when I saw a low, dark shape emerge from the waves. As I stood transfixed, it was joined by another, a little distance away, and then a third. My heart began to race with excitement at the realisation that an arribada was about to begin. I had managed to reach the right place at the right time!

Arribada is a Spanish word that means 'the arrival'. In Mexico and Costa Rica, two of the other countries where sea turtles gather to nest in the thousands, the arrival of the turtles once or twice a year used to be eagerly awaited by local people. They would collect tens of thousands of turtle eggs and sell them in the markets. This used to happen in Gahirmatha too, but no longer. Tonight, in this protected sanctuary, the turtles and their eggs were safe.

Each wave brought more than a dozen turtles to the shore. They paused in the surf, bodies glistening in the pale moonlight, before advancing up the beach like little Sherman Tanks. The turtles, all females, were coming ashore to lay their eggs in the sand. Each was about 80 cm long and weighed about 40 kilos, which is quite a bit of bulk to carry on land for an aquatic animal. A sea turtle's front legs are modified as flippers that are superb for swimming, but not much good for moving on land. Pausing every now and then to rest and take a breath, a female will laboriously haul her body up the beach slope until she reaches a flat surface well away from the high-tide line.

I decided to follow one female through the entire nesting process, a fascinating procedure that is almost identical in all the seven sea-turtles' species in the world. After making a shallow 'body pit' with her flippers, she dexterously began to scoop out a deep hole in the sand using her paddle-like hind legs. When the hole was about 45 cm deep, she settled down to lay her eggs. By carefully digging some sand away from her shell, I could crouch down with my torch and photograph the eggs being laid. First came one egg, followed by two more together, and then a flurry of three! I cupped my hand into the hole and caught the next one before it hit the ground. It was round, with a parchment-like shell, and just a little bit larger than a ping-pong ball. A coating of slightly sticky mucus cushioned its fall. During the next 15 minutes, the female laid over a hundred eggs, oblivious to the flashes from my camera.

A human presence on a beach will usually deter a turtle from coming ashore. But during arribadas, the females seem to throw all caution to the winds and are undeterred by the presence of humans, lights or camera flashes. Once a female begins to lay her eggs, however, she goes into a trance-like state, and even singing at the top of your voice or dancing like a maniac will not elicit the slightest reaction.

After she had laid all her eggs, 'my turtle' began closing up the nest. She pushed the sand back into the hole using her hind feet and pressed it down firmly. Then, she did something remarkable. Raising herself up on her flippers, she began to pound the sand with her plastron (the underside of a turtle's shell). She rocked her body from side-to-side, hitting the ground with force and packing the sand in the nest tighter and tighter. This thud of shell meeting sand can be heard from quite a distance away. By now, there were thousands of turtles all around me, in various stages of nesting, and the unearthly drumming could be heard from all sides. It was like a scene straight out of *The Lost World*! In fact, so crowded was the beach by then that many of the new arrivals were digging up earlier nests while making their own, tossing the others' eggs helter-skelter.

After pounding the sand to her satisfaction, the female used her flippers to toss dry sand over the nest to camouflage it. Then, she turned around and headed back to the sea, leaving her eggs in nature's care. She would have nothing more to do with them. The young, when they emerged 50 days later, would have to fend for themselves. I followed her all the way down to the sea and watched as she was swallowed up by the waves.

I stumbled around for the rest of the night, stubbing my toes on hard shells and getting rammed into by turtles coming in to nest or returning to the sea. Before I knew it, it was dawn. The sky turned pink, and the sun came up, revealing a beach etched with tractor-like turtle tracks as far as the eye could see.

Suddenly, the air was filled with the raucous squawking of sea gulls as a huge flock appeared from nowhere and descended on the beach to feast on the thousands of exposed eggs. Bone-tired but supremely happy, I continued my interrupted trek towards Chandrasekhar's camp, soon catching up with him and his team. They had been counting and tagging turtles all night and were as exhausted as I was. We trudged back to camp in companionable silence, to the hot breakfast and sweet tea that awaited us. Then I curled up in a corner of his tent and fell into a deep slumber.

In the evening, I walked back to the nesting area and was astonished to find the beach pristine once more. The wind had completely erased the tracks, and there wasn't a shred of evidence that one of the most amazing dramas of the natural world had played out on that very beach just the night before. Had I not witnessed it myself I would never have known that over a million eggs lay buried in the sand under my feet. I had wondered why the turtles had chosen such a windy night for nesting, and here appeared to be the answer! Amazing are the ways of nature.

## Fast Forward

Since my magical first visit to Gahirmatha in 1982, I have returned to Orissa several times, visiting not only Gahirmatha, but also the other mass-nesting beaches at the mouth of the Devi River and the mouth of the Rushukuliya River, respectively. Sadly, the olive ridleys have suffered a cruel fate during the intervening years and their plight continues with no respite in sight.

Alarmed by media reports of mass turtle deaths, I decided to investigate and make a documentary film on the subject. In 2001 and 2002, my colleague Shivakumar and I spent several months on the Orissa coast, often in the company of Biswajit

Mohanty of the Wildlife Society of Orissa and Dr Bivash Pandav, a sea-turtle biologist. What we witnessed was a needless carnage that was truly shocking: kilometres of coast littered with the rotting carcasses of adult olive ridleys. 'This is not a new sight,' Biswajit told us. 'Every year for the past few years we have counted over ten thousand carcasses on our beaches. We have repeatedly brought this to the notice of the concerned authorities but the government has simply turned a blind eye to this recurring tragedy.'

The turtles, all in their prime breeding years, were not dying of some mysterious disease, but were the accidental victims of uncontrolled mechanised fishing. Until the early 1980s, most sea fishing was done by artisanal fishermen in small, traditional fishing craft. The nets they used posed no threat to the turtles and it was extremely rare to see dead turtles on the beaches. But all that changed when, encouraged by advice from foreign experts, the state government imported a few mechanised trawlers. When these came back with huge catches of lucrative tiger prawns after every sortie, there was a mad scramble by businessmen to exploit the bounties of the ocean using modern technology. Loans and licences were issued with no regard to carrying capacity or potential ecological impacts, with disastrous consequences. From hardly any in the early 1980s, mechanised boat numbers had gone up to over 1,500 by 2002, a third of which, according to some estimates, plied without licences. Compounding the problem, many fishing vessels also encroach into the coastal waters of Orissa from neighbouring West Bengal and Andhra Pradesh. None of the boats heeded any of the marine fishing laws of the state, nor is there any significant enforcement.

A trawler drags a long, bag-like net behind it, which scoops up everything in the sea. When the net is full, it is winched aboard. Turtles found in the net, dead or alive, are tossed back into the sea. The ones still alive swim away while many of the dead ones eventually wash up on the beaches. Scientific studies have shown that not all dead turtles reach the shore. Many float on ocean currents until they start coming apart, and then sink to the bottom. So, the actual numbers that are being killed in Orissa and rest of the east coast is anybody's guess.

Sea turtles are air-breathers. They can hold their breaths for far longer than we can but they can't breathe underwater. When a turtle is caught in a net and forced to stay underwater for more than ninety minutes, it slips into unconsciousness. If held underwater for more than two hours, it dies. Bivash discovered that when kept on deck and protected from the sun, many comatose turtles miraculously revived after a few hours and were fit enough to be released back into the sea. But most trawl boat crews neither know this, nor care. In any case, there isn't much spare room on the deck of a trawl boat, so the turtles just get thrown overboard to drown.

Unlike in the coastal waters of other states, where turtle densities are low, the sea in Orissa teems with olive ridleys between November and April. The tragedy is that their arrival in Orissa from the Indian Ocean south of Sri Lanka coincides with the peak fishing season. Trawl nets often get so full of turtles that there is no room for fish in them. It's a no-win situation; loss of time and money for the trawl boat owners and a cruel and needless death for the turtles.

Another method of fishing that has been found to have a huge impact on turtles is known as gill netting. Gill nets are long, virtually invisible nets strung across the sea; some are as long as three kilometres. Swimming turtles get hopelessly entangled in these nets and die. When just one or two turtles are found dead in a net, the fishermen usually just chop off the head and flippers and thus remove them from the net. But when dozens of turtles get entangled at the same time, the net is invariably abandoned and cut adrift. This tangled mass floats around, trapping more and more turtles. In February 2002, a gill net that washed ashore on the Devi Beach had 205 dead turtles in it, mostly pregnant females.

Most of these annual deaths can be avoided. During his research, Bivash Pandav found that the olive ridleys that migrate to Orissa from the Indian Ocean do not spread out at random in the sea. Instead, they form three huge aggregations, known as reproductive patches, just offshore from the three mass-nesting beaches of Gahirmatha, Devi and Rushukuliya. It is quite easy to identify and plot the extent of these reproductive patches, which only occupy a small fraction of the available fishing area in the sea. If mechanised fishing boats simply kept away from these aggregations, it would benefit both the turtles and the boat owners tremendously. After all, repeatedly coming up with a trawl net full of turtles after four to five hours of trawling effort, or having to cut loose a highly expensive gill net represents a huge loss to the owner of the boat. Yet, despite the information about the reproductive patches being available for nearly a decade, this valuable insight has found no place in marine fishing policy in Orissa.

No one knows the size of the olive ridley population that visits Orissa to breed, but you don't need to be a rocket scientist to infer that the deaths of over 140,000 breeding adults (since 1999 when systematic counting of carcasses began) cannot but be catastrophic for a slow-maturing species.

While the state and central government in India have done precious little to tackle the needless annual carnage, the international sea turtle community too, has not taken the issue as seriously as it should, doing little beyond passing resolutions at conferences and seminars. Indeed, a few biologists have even gone so far as to assert that the death of over 10,000 breeding adults annually is not such a big deal. They argue that the olive ridley is the most numerous of the world's seven species of sea turtles, and is therefore, in no danger of going extinct in the near future. Sure, total extinction might be a long way away, but I have no doubt whatsoever that if the mindless slaughter continues, the incredible spectacle of tens of thousands of turtles nesting *en masse* will soon be a thing of the past in Orissa. And that would be a sad loss indeed. To me, the olive ridley arribada is a phenomenon that is no less important than the great wildebeast migration on the plains of Africa. Orissa's coastal waters and mass nesting beaches are our Serengetis. If we don't act now, one more of the great wonders of the natural world will disappear before our very eyes.

# Memories of Gir

*A.J.T. Johnsingh*

*Avid reading of Jim Corbett in Tamil inspired in Dr A.J.T. Johnsingh a yen for adventure and a love for the sights and sounds of the forest. He studied the Asiatic wild dog—which was the first study in India, by an Indian—on a free-ranging large mammal. He went on to become a wildlife biologist of great repute. He has roamed the remotest forests of the country (mainly on foot), with a camera and rod, and knows the rhythm and mystery of our forests like few others.*

*One of his key contributions to conservation is that he helped train over 300 wildlife managers, who now oversee protected areas in India and neighbouring countries.*

*Johnsingh has been instrumental in establishing a sanctuary for the rare grizzled squirrel, written many scientific papers and popular articles, and identified Kuno in Madhya Pradesh as a second home for the Asiatic lion. In this article, however, the author does not touch on the ongoing battle to shift the endangered Asiatic lion to an alternate home, or even the myriad threats it faces. Instead, he gives us a privileged peek into the secret life of the Asiatic lion in its only refuge, the Gir National Park in Gujarat.*

It was late January 1987, and I was perched on a tree, looking over a dry *nallah* criss-crossed with lion tracks. A goat kid had been tied in the *nallah* to attract lions, but the kid turned out to be a disappointment, as it fed quietly, refusing to call and raise an interest among the carnivores! There was no time to look for another site, and I therefore decided to wait till it was dark. The other members of my darting team waited, in a vehicle about 500 m away.

To my right, there lay a fairly open meadow, with lots of thorny trees like *Acacia senegal* and *A. nilotica*; a group of common langur was feeding in this patch. A footpath leading from the Acacia jungle went behind the tree on which I was sitting and the area was bathed in the soft evening light. At around 1700 hours, there were alarm calls from the langur, who jumped excitedly up and down on the thorny branches. I assumed a lion was approaching, and quickly took the dart gun, turned around and faced the trail with bated breath. Instead, there walked a leopard carrying a young langur in its mouth. Slowly, I replaced the gun on my lap, picked up my camera, focused, and clicked. The leopard, being much more alert than a lion, saw these movements, dropped the langur and ran away.

I continued to sit in the hide, hoping against hope that a lion would eventually amble past. Just as it was getting dark, my leopard came creeping up, one eye on the langur and the other on me, grabbed the langur, and ran away. The pictures that I took of this leopard remain some of my favourites . . .

Winter is the best period for large-mammal biologists to conduct field work in India, particularly in northern India. The winter months are free from the incessant drizzle and occasional downpour of the monsoon and the energy-sapping scorching heat and dust of the summer. Roads damaged by rains are usually repaired to become motorable by early winter. Weather conditions favourable to humans are also conducive to large mammals and as a result, animals are generally much more visible during the cool months. Winter is particularly suitable for drug immobilisation and radio-collaring, as the ambient temperatures are ideal for such operations. But, in places like Gir in Gujarat, one feels the winter only at night and early in the morning, because daytime temperatures are sometimes no pleasanter than those in summer.

That January, most of the faculty of the Wildlife Institute of India, diploma officer trainees, and several members of the Gujarat forest department were in Sasan Gir, with the purpose of radio-collaring lions. Dust flew off the roads in the mid-day heat, yellow and brown leaves fell from the trees and the withered nature of the jungle gave the impression that summer had already arrived. These conditions had not deterred Ravi Chellam, a researcher who had meticulously identified the lions that needed to be radio-collared. These included an adult male, an adult female and a sub-adult male near Sasan, and an adult male near Janwadla. The local forest staff fondly called the first adult male Dharam, after the robust film star Dharmendra. Dharam, with his equally robust partner, Veer, made up the most dominant male group around Sasan.

After several days of excellent teamwork, Dharam was eventually tranquilised with a mixture of ketamine hydrochloride and xylazine (Rompun), and radio-collared on 31 January, near the Kamaleshwar reservoir. The drug made him sick and he threw up the cattle meat which he had eaten a few hours earlier. Soon, he became used to the radio-collar, and thereafter Ravi had a marvellous time following the pair day and night over the

e Asiatic black bear inhabits broad-leaved and coniferous forests usually between 00 to 3,000 metres.

Prerna Singh Bindra

e Hanuman langur (left) is known for its unique association with the cheetal (above), who eats fruits and leaves dropped by the langur. They also warn each other of any approaching predators.

A tusker in Similipal Tiger Reserve, before the attack by Maoists in March 2009, anc
the damaged forest-department staff-quarters (below) in Chahala, in the heart of
reserve.

Prerna Singh Bindra

Prerna Singh Bindra

Peter Jackson with the legendary 'Birdman' of India, Dr Salim Ali.

Defenders of the wild: Patrolling the Sundarbans Tiger Reserve.

: Arunachal macaque, one of the highest-dwelling primates of the world, was covered in 2003.

: population of the slender-billed vulture has seen a sudden crash — about percent — in the past decade.

Kalyan Varma

The rainforests of the Western Ghats host a number of endemic species.

Mohit Aggarwal

hills and valleys of western Gir. The lions' kingdom ranged over an area of about 150 sq km east, north and south of Sasan, an area rich in chital and sambar. Following Dharam and Veer, and some other lions, Ravi studied the major difference between the social organisation of lions in Gir and Serengeti (in Africa).

The Gir male coalition groups attached themselves to female groups only when one or two females were in heat, or when the female group was on a large kill, like a buffalo. This is adaptive for the lions as the principal prey of female groups in Gir is chital, which, on an average, weighs 40 kg. If the males, who dominate over the kills, eating 20–30 kg when they are hungry, are always with the females, there will be very little food left for the females and the cubs. The easy availability of the not-so-agile cattle also enables the males not to depend entirely on the females for food. Detached from the female groups, the male groups wander from one habitat patch to another, looking for food and females in estrous, and warning off the neighbouring male groups with their periodic roars.

Veer and Dharam found strength and courage in one another's company. They fought many battles with adjacent male groups and always won, albeit with the loss of some mane hair and a few ghastly wounds. In August 1987, however, Veer was killed by some local people and this had a disastrous effect on Dharam. The brave Dharam became a fugitive in his own kingdom; his range shrunk, he stopped roaring, lost his mane and began to resemble a large female. He was seldom found in the riverine tracts, which are the favoured haunts of lions during the hot hours of the day. He died eventually, possibly of hunger (and maybe, out of loneliness and fear); Ravi found only his withered body reduced to a bag of skin and bones.

At Dehradun, the rest of us waited for the next winter to resume our radio-collaring operations. In November 1988, we were in Gir again. This time our first camp was at the Kankai temple, as we planned to radio-collar lions in central Gir. Before leaving Sasan, we had bought nearly 50 kg of raw groundnut, freshly harvested from the fields around Gir, and our *modus operandi* was as follows: early in the morning, we boiled 7–8 kg of groundnuts in salt water, put this in a gunny bag, and left for the jungle. The groundnuts, the abundant *ber* fruits (*Zizyphus mauritiana*), water from any one of the streams, and occasional buttermilk from a maldhari ness, sustained us throughout the day. At night, in the Kankai temple, the priests gave us a liberal supper of *bajra roti* with some dry brinjal curry.

But this life was not without incident. After several days of such hardship, we were woken one morning by Ravi's moaning, and we found him in a delirium. We gave him hot water to drink, made him swallow whatever medication we had for fever, and covered him with all our sleeping bags. But the fever did not subside till the evening, and Ravi continued to shiver and moan. I left Ravi in the care of Jamal, and drove to Sasan 30 km away, to send the local medical doctor to Kankai, who immediately left with the necessary medicines. I finished some shopping and left for Kankai at around 2100 hours. On the way back, I met the doctor returning from Kankai, and he told me that he had medicated Ravi, leaving him sleeping fitfully when he left an hour ago. Ravi would be well enough to continue field work the next day! I thanked him profusely, and before parting, asked him casually what animals he had seen while returning from Kankai. He replied (even more casually) that he had seen four leopards: one solitary, and a mother with two cubs. Gir, apart from its obviously hallowed status as a lion habitat, is one of the finest leopard habitats in our country.

Plenty of lion tracks, old and new, along the banks of Sudavi River, indicated that this area was heavily used by lions. Sudavi ness is six km north of Chodavadi in central Gir. Seeing the abundant lion tracks, we decided to concentrate our efforts on radio-collaring one lion near Sudavi. We reached Sudavi early the next morning, and were greeted by chital alarm calls along the river bank. Could it be that the lions were hunting? We selected a fairly open plateau near the river, and tied a buffalo calf in the middle of the plateau. I climbed a *Wrightia tinctoria* tree, about 15 m east of the bait, and sat on a bare branch 5–6 metres above the ground. I was confident that if I didn't move, the lions wouldn't see me.

We had made a good choice of bait. As soon as the others left, the calf, unaware of my presence on the tree, started calling. This was quickly followed by langur and chital alarms in the east, hardly 500 m from me. After a few minutes, a pair of sambar bellowed, and bolted to the river on my left. Within seconds, I heard rustling sounds in the bushes behind.

I turned my head slowly and looked behind. Several lions were advancing through the bushes. The prime lioness came to the edge of the bushes, about 30 m from the calf, ran forward from right under my tree and killed the calf. I waited for a few seconds, took careful aim at the left shoulder of the lioness, and fired. With a growl, the lioness ran 10–15 m from the kill with the dart stuck in her shoulder. Meanwhile, the other members of the pride, two adult lionesses and three one-year-old cubs, joined her. Although my tree had scanty leaf cover, they failed to see me, as the morning sun was right behind me. Then, in a wonderful display of power, the pride tugged at the kill, broke the rope, and disappeared with the kill into the dense scrub on the bank of the river.

Ten minutes later, giving sufficient time for the drug to act, my team members began to shout loudly for several minutes, so that the other lions would retreat, before they began a thorough search for the darted lioness. However, in spite of our best efforts, we could not locate the animal. Dr P.K. Malik, a veterinary doctor who had just joined the institute, said that this ought not to worry us much, as carnivores can metabolise the ketamine–xylazine drug easily.

It was now close to mid-day. Since we expected the lions to return to the kill in the evening, we dragged it closer to a dense *Zizyphus mauritiana* tree and tied it to a sapling. We had fabricated a cot-like structure with poles and coir rope to weigh the lions. This, I tucked into the canopy of the *Z. mauritiana* tree, climbed up the tree and told everybody to go and have lunch and come back in the evening. Before leaving, Ravi said that he would leave the three assistants about 200 metres away, so that they could be called if I needed their assistance to radio-collar a lion.

My hide was cool and comfortable. There were many ripe fruits within reach, I had a book to read, and the loaded dart-gun and camera were within reach. Around 13:30, the cawing of a large-billed crow got my attention, and I saw an adult lioness slowly approaching the kill. Ravi had told me that the Gir lions do not mind wandering about in the mid-day sun looking for food. When she reached the kill, she stood around for a few seconds, giving me ample time to take a few photographs. But, I was in a bit of a dilemma. Should I dart the lioness or not? Eventually, I fired. The dart went home and was embedded in the right shoulder of the lioness. She leaped over the kill, ran under my tree and disappeared into the deep *nallah* behind. I listened carefully, trying to locate where she had gone, from the growling, rolling and jumping sounds. Finally, there was silence.

I whistled to the assistants and they came to the edge of the clearance. Using sign language, they asked me whether they should approach me. I waved to them to come and got down, with their assistance, from my thorny hide. When I explained to them in my broken Hindi what had happened, one of them ran back to the place where they had been resting, brought a radio-collar and the other equipment. Thereafter, within a matter of minutes, the animal was found and radio-collared. I got back up my hide hoping to take more pictures of lions, and the assistants went back to their resting site. It was a totally perplexed and happy Ravi who came to the tree to greet me, when the assistants briefed him of the events that occurred in his absence.

The Chodavadi female, which had an annual home range of about 120 sq km, later provided Ravi with excellent information. In the dry season, the female and her group, averaging five animals, were largely confined to the dry riverine tracts. Although Ravi recorded 109 locations for this female, only once was she seen with an adult male, confirming the very weak social bonds between the resident pride females and the resident territorial males.

Our radio-collaring programme in November 1988 was very successful.

Another year passed before I could go to Gir again, in November 1989. This time, we decided to radio-track the Leria (eastern Gir) male, which had an annual range of 230 sq km. Ravi regularly followed different lions for whole days with the help of his assistants. Dhananjai Mohan, an Indian Forest Service probationer (now a brilliant forest officer), was also with us. Sometime late in the evening, when it was about to get dark, we located the Leria male with his male coalition partner. As we started to track him, a thin fog enveloped the forest, dimming the light of the young moon and stars. Ravi drove the open jeep, Dhananjai sat at the edge of the front seat, and I stood in the middle, radio-tracking. The males moved along the road, from one ness to another, probably looking for old and sick cattle left out by the Maldharis at night. They roared as they went past a ness. We followed them slowly in the dim light of the moon. A sambar bellowed in a *nallah* hardly 50 m from the road, but the lions did not show any interest in the large deer. They obviously knew that there was easier prey available.

When the males entered the forest, we drove ahead of them, turned the vehicle around, and stood facing the direction from which they were coming. We had parked the vehicle on a bridge, the distance between the jeep and the left wall of the bridge being about five metres. Only one male came along the road and we sat and watched silently. The lion first went to the wall, probably sprayed it, and then, out of curiosity, walked to the jeep on our left. As the lion came closer, Dhananjai leaned as far as possible to my side, pressing hard against my legs, but did not scream. The lion almost touched the jeep and then walked away without even looking at us. After the lion had gone ahead by 50 m, we allowed ourselves to break into excited laughter, thrilled with this encounter.

Lions do not walk or hunt throughout the night; at times they also take a nap. Around 0200 hours, the radio signals indicated that the lions were resting, and by experience, Ravi knew that this resting would last probably two hours. Therefore, we also decided to rest and the only place available was the road. As the night was bitterly cold, we built a fire, spread our sheets on the ground around the fire, and slept. At around 0300 hours we heard roaring and growling from the direction of the lions, which were about 500 m from us, up the road. The lions were fighting. We sat up on our sheets and watched as a male came running by, chased by another male; both ran past just 10 m from us. Ravi figured that another male had possibly come close to the resting pair, and had been chased away.

Back in Chodavadi, at around 0400 hours, on an extremely cold winter morning, dewdrops glistened brightly on the grass. Ravi was driving and I was sitting at the edge of the front seat of the jeep, with my camera and flash ready, hoping to get a picture of either a leopard or lion. In my drowsiness that morning, I had not spotted the improper alignment between the flash and the speed of the camera. We noticed a small animal, like a jungle cat, sitting on the road. Ravi said, 'Sir, there's the kitten of a jungle cat. You can take a picture.' I got off the jeep and took three or four pictures of the cat shivering in the cold. I did notice that the little animal was rusty brown in colour and spotted heavily. Nevertheless, I did not realise that I was possibly taking the first picture of a rusty spotted cat in the wild. The slides were soon tucked away into an almirah and forgotten.

Many months later, I received a copy of *Hornbill,* a magazine published by the Bombay Natural History Society, and it had a marvellous picture of a rusty spotted cat taken by Bharat Pathak, a devoted and capable forest officer from Gujarat. Bharat had seen the cat sitting up in a small tree in Gir, on one of his night drives. He identified the picture with the help of scientists at the BNHS and their valuable skin collection of the many wild animals that occur on the Indian subcontinent.

My memories of Gir are full of lions, leopards, hyenas, and the nimble-footed chousingha and chinkara. I can only hope that pilgrimages to numerous temples in the protected region will not grow out of control. Or, that demands for more cement in the industrial state of Gujarat will not force the government to denotify portions of Gir that are rich in deposits of limestone. I also hope that the prosperous sugar cane cultivation around this protected area will not sap the underground freshwater, turning it into a saline wasteland. As suggested by Diwakar Sharma of the Wildlife Institute of India, teak trees in the park, which have little forage value, should be thinned to create more grasslands for the ungulates. Gir should also ideally be totally free of all humans, including Maldharis. But they should be given an alternate site, plentiful in water and forage and the resettlement of Maldharis should be carried out slowly, over decades, as lions still get substantial amount of their food from livestock. . . . Gir should, in fact, be home only to Asiatic lions, leopards and many more rusty spotted cats and their prey.

First published in *Sanctury Asia*, Vol. XXIII, December 2003
Written with inputs from Dr Ravi Chellam

# A Pest is Born

*RANJIT LAL*

*Ranjit Lal, a keen naturalist, has written extensively for various newspapers and magazines. He has authored a number of books, including those with charmingly quirky titles such as* Life and Times of Altu Faltu, The Crow Chronicles *and* The Caterpillar Who Went on a Diet, *besides his latest offering,* Wild City: Natural Wonders Next Door. *Ranjit opens a window to another world. While most of us, even those passionate about nature, are obsessed with the glamour of mega fauna; Ranjit makes much of smaller creatures that one tends to largely ignore or view as 'pests', such as the caterpillar in this featured story. He writes with much fondness and attention to detail about the various birds, animals and insects he encounters, almost making one wonder whether he occupies the same space as we do. This one may seem like an oddball—a work of fiction on the making of a butterfly, but the author has the gift of making what appears to be mundane, fascinating.*

No one, not even someone with a nature-obsession, would look twice at a bird-dropping on a leaf unless it did something really extraordinary.

And, the one I was staring at was doing precisely that. It was, in fact, devouring the leaf it had been 'dropped on'. The leaf in question belonged to the Chinese orange plant that lived outside the front door, where I waited for the doorbell to be answered. Closer examination of this animated bird-dropping revealed it to be a caterpillar and everything was explained. Birds adore juicy caterpillars, but which self-respecting bird would dare eat (or be seen eating) a bird-dropping, even if it knew fully well that the dropping could well turn out to be a juicy caterpillar.

Nature is wickedly ingenious.

Of course, I knew that butterflies laid eggs, which hatched into caterpillars, which became pupae (or chrysalises), which turned into butterflies, but I thought it might be interesting to see this actually happen. So, I incarcerated the bird-dropping alias caterpillar in a jam jar along with a generous supply of leaves (of its food plant, it would touch no other) and began to watch it assiduously.

It was both fascinating and revolting. The caterpillar would launch these frantic gastronomic orgies from time to time, demolishing half a leaf in five minutes—the equivalent of you gobbling up a *parantha* the size of a dining table! Bouts of gobbling would be interspersed with bouts of introspection (and burping, I would imagine, though I never heard any) as though it were regretting its last round of excesses. But then, back it would go to bingeing. Naturally, it put on weight; after three or four days it was large and brave enough to shed its infra dig bird-dropping disguise, and emerged in a neat leaf-green suit complete with two large fake 'eyes' near its head (to make it look fearsome and snake-like). Now, it merged perfectly into its leafy environment.

Its appetite increased prodigiously and you could now actually hear its wasp-coloured jaws rasp up and down the edges of leaves. In the meantime, I had read up a bit about these particular caterpillars and they were agricultural history-sheeters all right, pests of citrus orchards. They were caterpillars of the lemon-leaf butterfly, a member of the glamorous swallow-tail family. A further examination of the Chinese orange plant yielded a few tiny pearl-like spherical eggs, from which these eating machines emerged. After hatching, the minuscule caterpillar's first act was to eat the eggshell, not in order to destroy evidence of its existence, but to obtain vital sustenance contained therein.

In nature nothing is wasted. Another lesson wasted on us. . . .

I also found out that, proportionally, caterpillars eat much more than elephants (forget about sumo-wrestlers). If elephants ate (proportionately) as much as caterpillars, they would defoliate the world and produce vast amounts of dung in terms of tonnage per day per head. My lemon-leaf caterpillar shot pellets of dung (called frass) far away from itself, probably so that it wouldn't give itself away.

By choice it was a nocturnal gastronome. During the day, it would usually arrange itself along the midrib of a leaf and pretend to be just that. By night, it would devour that leaf (and others), and then pretend to be the midrib of another leaf the next morning. If you irritated it (by blowing gently on it), it would rear up and flick two blood-red filamentous antennae, like protrusions (called osmaterium), from the top of its head. These are apparently supposed to impersonate the flickering forked tongue of a snake, and emit an unpleasant odour. On a later occasion, when two hefty green caterpillars met head on, on the same twig, they reared up and snapped their jaws together and flickered their snakes' tongues warningly, before backing off. Perhaps, they have some kind of snake fetish and believe that if they look and behave like serpents, they'll be left well alone!

Anyway, the caterpillar stuffed itself solidly for about a week, growing larger, thicker and more handsome by the day. Occasionally, it would pause to split out of its skin (when it grew too tight), but it always had a brand new and elastic one on underneath. Then, at last, it decided to give up the good things of life and take up a monastic existence. It affixed its nether end—where its claspers were located—to a twig, with the help of a sticky silk pad, and slung a silken girdle around the upper end of its body, arranging itself hammock-like along the twig. Then it went into a coma, curling up and twitching occasionally. That evening it split its caterpillar skin again, and for the last time, to reveal a perfect leaf-green pupa or chrysalis beneath. With a deft flick, the old caterpillar skin was 'kicked' off as the hind end of the pupa detached and re-attached itself to the twig in a jiffy. Here, it would now remain, immobile and hopefully undetected, until the magic taking place inside it was complete. (I later discovered that caterpillars had yet another trick up their sleeves to escape detection: the pupae that developed during the monsoon month of August were leaf-green and merged perfectly with their verdant surroundings; those that developed after the monsoons, in October were bark-brown so as to merge with the drier autumnal foliage.)

Unfortunately, you can't see the miracle that takes place inside the pupa. Caterpillars are apparently equipped with two basic kinds of cells. One type is geared exclusively to the gluttonous consumption of leaf tissue. These cells do not subdivide as cells normally do when a living creature grows, but instead simply increase in size and mass as the caterpillar ingests leaf after leaf, until it is several thousand times its original size. The second group of cells, clustered in dense groups, lie dormant and bide their time during this stage, not developing at all. For they contain within them, the blueprint of the final product—the butterfly. Once the pupa is formed, however, these cells take their cue and go into action. For now, the gigantic caterpillar cells die and break down into a gravy or soup, which provides nourishment for the hitherto dormant butterfly cells. These now begin to subdivide in the normal way, and form various parts of the insect: the delicate slim legs, the beautiful dappled wings and the dark, expressive eyes.

Eight days after the chrysalis had formed, I knew that the butterfly was due to emerge. The rich green of the pupa had ebbed away into transparency and I could see the insect's dark, polka-dotted body through it, as well as the tightly rolled-up (umbrella fashion) wings. As butterflies are usually born early, I set the alarm for 4 a.m. the next morning, and hoped I wouldn't be too late.

For two and a half sleepy hours the next morning, I watched the pupa twitch and buck as the butterfly inside made final preparations for its entry into the world. At last, at around 6.30 a.m., it gave a couple of convulsive heaves and partially split open the chrysalis laterally, midway across its length. One at a time, the delicate insect extracted its spindly legs from the broken pupal husk (like someone climbing out of a canoe), wearing a section of the husk over its head like a helmet (which I gently removed). Eventually, it pulled away from the dried-up chrysalis and crawled tiredly up the twig to spread and dry its wings. The wings, so crumpled and crushed, began to expand and flatten as the butterfly pumped blood through the fine network of veins. Once the wings are fully extended, the blood is drawn back into the insect's body, and the veins dry and harden into struts, providing a framework for the wings. If, by chance, the butterfly is not able to unfurl and hang down its wings fully, or if they are snagged, they will set in their crumpled state, crippling the insect for life.

I watched it now with wonder; this freshly minted beautiful creature that had once, in its hideous past, impersonated a bird-dropping and been a ravenous glutton. For the rest of its life it would dither skittishly over flowers and fussily sip nectar.

Its eyes were large and lustrous, as black and soft as jet. Being compound eyes, they receive a multitude of separate images, enabling the butterfly to see the world as a complex mosaic of tiny pictures.

The proboscis, curled tightly as a watch-spring, occasionally uncoiled tentatively. Through this hair-fine tube, the insect would suck up nectar, water and less delicate substances like the juices from rotting meat and fruit, mud (for minerals), and the moisture from dung. Its club-tipped antennae, feeling the air cautiously, would be used for balance in flight, and is acutely sensitive to smell. The wings, dappled in lemon and black, with crayon smudges in saffron and mauve, opened and shut gently as they dried. Covered with hundreds of tile-like, racquet-shaped scales, they are coloured with pigments (in this case, the yellow and orange), or reflect light, which gives rise to the metallic shimmering blues in some species. Amongst those normal scales, lie some specialised scent scales (only the males have these) which produce an aphrodisiac to excite the female during courtship. The male flutters madly around the female, in order to 'spray' his seductive scent around her. However, it is the female who actually summons the male hither; she produces a highly seductive perfume (these substances are called pheromones) from the tip of her abdomen which is so powerful that it lures males from miles around towards her.

Still, the butterfly rested; never would this insect be as perfect as it was during that hour after its birth. For once it was in the big wide world, it would be buffeted by the wind and snapped at by birds and lizards. If it survived, it would scatter its seductive perfume, attract a partner, mate, and if female, touch-dance over the Chinese orange and lay its pearl-like eggs. And then, it would die, its mission in life complete.

In this event, my lemon-leaf butterfly lived perhaps for little more than an hour. I had left it in the balcony, still resting on its twig, and had gone in for a bath. When I emerged I found it in tatters on the floor, with my boxer chops swiping at it interrogatively with his paws. It had probably fluttered enticingly past his nose, and that was that.

I've seen butterflies hatch several times subsequently (with less tragic results) and have never failed to be wonderstruck. It is really astonishing to see something so beautiful and perfect emerge out of a past so filled with gluttony.

If only such a fate could befall our own species.

First published in *Mostly Birds, Some Monkeys and a Pest*,
published by Ravi Dayal Publishers, in 2000.

# A Letter to Teddy

*Amit Chaudhery*

*This isn't a pretty story, but then the fate of wild bears isn't either – killed and milked for their bile, or captured alive to dance to our tunes. What follows is a profoundly moving story, or more accurately, a letter penned by a cursed Mama Bear to her cub. This is culled from* Voices in My Head, *a compilation of distressingly realistic and powerful pieces that speaks of the plight of animals. Amit Chaudhery has also authored a book on the television and broadcasting industry. Chaudhery worked as an advertising copywriter and a broadcast journalist before his present occupation as a communications specialist. He has been widely published in newspapers and magazines, is a folk historian, and is closely involved with animal rights issues.*

Dear Teddy,

I am writing to you from Faraway. This letter comes on the Wings of Intent; read it and make a promise never to forget. Ever.

I know you wonder where I am. I know you weep. You must be angry too, at my not returning home with the promised honey hive for your birthday. I wish I could change the situation, Ted. But this is a luxury God denied us. We must accept what comes our way, silently.

Let me tell you what happened.

I had gone out that morning in Spring to search for the largest honey hive in the great forest. My baby deserves the best, I told myself. Besides, I wanted to see you dip your head into the pod only to raise it, as treacle-thick honey dripped lazily down your little face and your pink tongue chased it in eager haste, as it always did when you ate at home. Well, I searched and searched till I found what I felt sure was the biggest and best honey hive. I was heading back to you and your excited baby talk, when I decided to walk over to the top of the Wishing Mountain for daisies. What's a birthday without flowers, I asked myself. Besides, they always looked lovely behind your ears.

The Wishing Mountain proved to be my death wish. I was plucking the last flower, when something—I still don't know what—knocked me out. I woke up to find myself in an Iron Dragon* racing downhill. It was pitch dark; so dark that I was

---

*Bear word for automobile.

unable to see my paw even if I held it before my face. I was groggy, hungry, sore and frightened. Very frightened. When the Iron Dragon opened its mouth to sunlight, He threw a net over me and dragged me out, before beating me unconscious. I was tied to a chain and kept without food till the sun drove his chariot across the sky seven times. It was then, when I felt close to death, that my 'lessons' began.

He pulled out my claws with pincers, strapped a tight muzzle over my mouth after drilling a hole through the roof of my mouth. Then, He taught me to 'dance'. On hot metal plates, as my feet burned to a crisp, I had to dance, Teddy, because I had to lift each foot turn by turn, to temporarily escape the searing heat. I had to dance, because He pulled hard (at a noose which went through the roof of my mouth) if I made a wrong step. I danced the Dance of Hell to become what I am now: A Dancing Bear.

I am led by Him through the great filth of His jungle called The City, as His children jeer at me. I am fed scraps, but most nights I sleep hungry in the lap of exhaustion. The beatings continue as He heaps his black sadism on me.

I am lucky, He says. Bears are baited, too. Tied to a stake by a short chain as dogs bite and snap in a bloody merry-go-round. I am lucky, He tells me. Bears are sent to Bear Farms to be confined in cages so small we can't move or even sit up straight, as crude pipes inserted into our bellies draw out bile juice. Drop, by painful drop.

Perhaps, a lifetime of degradation and abuse is better than being farmed or baited.

Don't think you are safe Ted, even though you are less than six-moons-old. He steals children, too. And eats them in Bear Banquets, slowly drowning Bear Babies in scalding water, after spending time leisurely, choosing which child to make a meal of from behind polished glass windows in exotic restaurants.

Be very careful, your first mistake would be your last. Nothing we know or do can get the better of Him. As for me, I'll dance my life away. Love for you etched on my heart forever.

Mama Bear

NOTE: Teddy never received this letter. The Wings of Intent are strong, bur not strong enough to get past 'polished glass windows in exotic restaurants.' The letter bounced off the windows to become a precise arrowhead. Ricocheting off its failed mission, it pierced Mama Bear's breast, who then died of a broken heart.

Excerpted from *Voices in My Head,* Banyan Books, 1998

# The Mating Tusker

*BIVASH PANDAV*

*Dr Bivash Pandav started his career as a wildlife biologist by studying olive ridley turtles in the Orissa coast, but the 'Turtle Man' of India has moved on since then. For the past five years, he has worked extensively in the Rajaji-Corbett landscape in the foothills of the western Himalayas, studying the big cats. Elephants are part of the Terai landscape as well, and in 'The Mating Tusker', the author reveals some inexplicable facets of elephant behaviour. The story poignantly brings out how these gentle giants, once worshipped as Ganesha, are now being killed, as the conflict between man and elephant escalates.*

*A close observer and a staunch defender of the wild, Bivash is an optimist and believes that there is still enough scope for tigers to make a comeback in many places across India. Unlike most countries across the tiger's range, India still has forested tracts that can host good populations of tigers and its prey. Bivash has published many scientific papers, written popular articles and currently coordinates the Tiger and Other Big Cats unit of South Asia for WWF International.*

I first saw him on a cold evening in January 2005. Winter was at its peak in the foothills of the Himalayas. Assisted by my colleague Karthik Vasudevan, two of our students, Amir Kurien and Abishek Harihar, and field assistant Imam Hussain, we were setting up camera traps deep inside the forest in the Chilla Range of the Rajaji National Park.

It was as routine as routine could be in the wilds, but all of a sudden we saw a cow elephant, followed by a bull, moving at a trot towards us.

Seeing the two elephants, apparently a courting pair, we ran towards the safety of our open Jeep, parked on the nearby forest road. I held a wetted thumb up to the wind to check the direction of the wind. The gentle breeze was blowing directly from us to the elephants and there was no way that the elephants had not detected our presence. We sat huddled quietly in the jeep, hoping we are not going to be taught a lesson in elephant etiquette. The elephants stood still for quite some time, till the tusker began to get on with the original task on hand and approached the cow elephant. I love elephants, but was more than a little relieved when they slowly moved away from us. We continued to watch the amorous pair and could now clearly hear other members of the herd snapping off branches as they fed on a nearby hill slope. By now, the tusker had positioned himself behind the cow elephant, ready to mount. By the time he actually started to mount, the elephants from the slope, perhaps on receiving an infrasonic communication from the female, rushed down, trumpeting and blowing air through their trunks. Incredibly, they circled the mating pair. The tusker dismounted after about a minute and the cow joined the group, which moved on towards the thickets . . . passing us one-by-one.

Why, I wondered, why did the female elephants circle the pair, almost as though part of a ritual. I have no answers.

By this time, I had positioned myself amidst of tall *Saccharum spontaneum* (Kaans) grass on the bank of the Mundal *sot* not far from the jeep. Soon, the tusker came towards the *sot* and stood in an open area on the forest road 40 metres or so from me. I could see him clearly. He was around 35 years of age and stood a bit under three metres at the shoulder. His thick tusks were slightly divergent, he had a sloping back and his tail extended till the ankle with a 'half-fish tail brush'. His overall posture presented a very calm and graceful demeanour. As I took photographs of him, little did I know that I would have several more encounters with the 'Mating Tusker', as we fondly named him, in the months ahead.

The forests of Chilla are located on the east bank of river Ganga and are connected with other parts of the Rajaji National Park on the west bank of the river, along a narrow corridor between Motichur and Chilla forests. A number of problems beset this Chilla–Motichur corridor that stretches across four islands between the two banks and efforts to restore the corridor have not been fully successful. Way back in 1987, a team of biologists from the Wildlife Institute of India (WII), led by Dr A.J.T. Johnsingh, evaluated the wildlife value of this corridor and came up with valuable recommendations. As part of WII's ongoing research programme in the Rajaji National Park, Karthik and I were here to re-evaluate the extent to which this corridor is still used by wildlife, and document the changes that have taken place over the last 18 years.

Winter was drawing to an end when we started field data collection in the corridor. In winter and spring, the water level in the snow-fed Ganges between Rishikesh and Haridwar, is at the lowest. The diversion of water in the form of a barrage near Rishikesh to the Chilla power channel further decreases the water level in the Ganga along this stretch. This low water level enabled us to frequently cross the river and get on to the islands that form a bulk of the corridor area.

On one lovely spring morning, while we were quantifying vegetation on one of the islands, we heard sound of branches being broken. The wind was blowing from the direction of the sound towards us and we carefully moved towards the sound.

Amidst the thick *Lantana* and *Canabis* bushes and the dense foliage of *Trewia nudifloralocal* (Gutail) trees, we saw a tusker. Anticipating that it would cross the nearby vast open area, we quickly moved on the edge of the opening and waited.

As expected, the magnificent elephant soon came out in the open and I noticed the characteristic half-fish tail brush. The tusk pattern and sloping back were the prefect identification marks of my old friend, the 'Mating Tusker'. Sensing our presence, he quickly moved away from us, but not before I managed to shoot a few frames.

A week later, early in the day after crossing the Ganges, we sat on a boulder taking in the warmth of the morning sun. Imam was the first to see the tusker getting into the river. The sun was against us and since all we would get was a silhouette, we took no pictures, preferring to observe the lord of this jungle. He had his fill of water before crossing the river to disappear into the Chilla forests.

I was lucky to observe him several times at close quarters, and while he had ample opportunity to charge, and show me my place in the scheme of things . . . he didn't. He never showed any sign of aggression. His reaction on seeing me was invariably to raise his tail and rapidly move away.

After a few encounters, I began to understand a bit more about the tusker's daily movement pattern. Through the day, he preferred to stay in the dense riverine forests along the east bank of the Ganga in the Chilla Range. Come evening, he invariably crossed the river and headed towards Motichur, across the islands. Wheat and sugarcane crops in winter, and mango in summer lured him towards the habitation near Motichur on an almost daily basis. Possibly, after foraging in the vicinity of Motichur, he would return to the Chilla forest between 6–7 a.m., crossing the Ganga at a specific location.

After one such encounter with the tusker, I spoke to Dr Johnsingh, who was worried that the tusker would probably not live long if he continued to frequent such predictable territory. The right bank of the Ganga on the western side of Rajaji NP was subject to many pressures and human presence—and the tuskers would not be welcome.

I was taken aback and hoped that he was wrong. In the past few years, the habitat has been making a rapid recovery and wildlife populations are bouncing back after the relocation of the Gujjars from the Chilla Range. Being quite optimistic about the future of large mammals in the area, and brimming with confidence about the future of wildlife in this tract, I ignored Dr Johnsingh's ominous prediction.

By June, the temperature soared to 45°C in the bhabar forests of Uttaranchal. The intense heat and the delayed monsoon had made conditions really tough for the wildlife of Chilla. Forest fires were commonplace and by 9 a.m., the entire area was like a furnace.

I waited for the tusker one morning in mid-June at his regular river crossing site. As if keeping an appointment, he appeared on the other bank of the river and came straight towards me. His tusks glowed in the soft morning light and I took several photographs. On reaching the shore and seeing me, as always, he lifted his tail and ran towards the jungle. At the time, I had no inkling that this would be my last glimpse of this splendid animal.

The monsoon winds finally brought the much-needed cooling rain to the foothills of the Himalayas in the last week of June. I was in Orissa, taking a break from work, when a phone call in the first week of July, brought devastating news. G.S. Pande, the director of Rajaji, informed me that on 5 July 2005 the tusker had crossed Ganga as usual and moved towards the west bank, never to return again.

Over the years, numerous ashrams have mushroomed all along the west bank from Motichur to Haridwar over the years. The huge mango orchards within the ashram premises are a major attraction for elephants. In all probability, alarmed by the regular visits of the tusker, people here had electrified the barbed wire fence along an orchard on the tusker's regular route. The procedure is simple enough. Steal electricity from an adjacent power line with a hook and a wire and connect it to the metal wire fence. The electric shock would have resulted in a massive heart attack. And that was the end of the 'Mating Tusker'. The end of this magnificent specimen, well over 4,000 kg, was sculpted by the hands of 'religious' people living in the holy town of Haridwar. A villager had tipped the authorities about a dead tusker lying within the premises of an ashram. The ashram people had quickly removed the barbed wire fencing and even tried to cover the elephant with a huge polythene sheet and mango boxes.

Park authorities seized the barbed wire, arrested the religious head and three others. The ashram head, however, secured bail and promptly left the country 'to give a religious discourse' abroad while the other three were taken to judicial custody.

One out of the ten identified adult bull tuskers from our study area was gone forever. Will the gods of Haridwar and Rishikesh come to the rescue of the remaining elephants, who continue to live under the twin threats of poaching and conflict? If I were one of those gods, I would never forget or forgive my worshippers for destroying what I had so carefully nurtured on Earth for thousands of years. Elephants are ancient creatures and their origin dates back to over 50 million years . . . and it is terrifying to think that creatures that we worshipped as gods are pitched against man for their very survival.

My only consolation is the fact that the 'Mating Tusker's' genes might live through the herds he lived close to. And my job has to see that there are forests left intact for such young elephants to roam about when we have passed.

First published in *Sanctuary Asia*, Vol. XXVI, February 2006

# Gabbar Singh and Chomsky in Dalma

*Dhriti K. Lahiri Choudhury*

*Dr Dhriti Lahiri Choudhury had a charming childhood in a near-mythic feudal world of royal food, classical music, shikar, and of course, household elephants. His family had seventeen elephants, which perhaps explains his passion for the pachyderm, and even after studying English at the Rabindra Bharati University in Kolkata, he travelled the forests of India—to the remotest of regions—in the quest of the elephant. He has watched and observed elephants for over seventy years, pursued man-killing rogues in far-flung forests, surveyed their status and distribution, studied the man–elephant conflict and the issues concerning their conservation. He was a member of the Asian Elephant Specialist Group of the International Union for Conservation of Nature. He edited* The Great Indian Elephant Book *and authored* A Trunk Full of Tales: Seventy Years with the Indian Elephant. *This story is a true reflection of the author's style, written with humour, a bit of irony and not without empathy and affection for the subject, even as Gabbar Singh, the hero of this tale, traumatises the good doctor and makes light of his expertise.*

They called him Gabbar Singh after the villain-hero of the film *Sholay,* the aggressive, firebrand tusker of Dalma, about thirty years old, beautifully built, with symmetrical tusks of medium length, always ready to take on anything that crossed his path, man or vehicle—a *mastan* if ever there was one. We knew him only as a loner, but no doubt he picked up his girlfriends now and then from the family groups moving around.

Mr S.P. Shahi, for long years the head of the forest department of Bihar, met him in Dalma in 1979. By then Mr Shahi had been well and truly bitten by the camera bug, and had exchanged his rifle for a Nikon F2. He had also had a heart attack by then which he was wont to take as a minor impediment to his wildlife activities. Mr Shahi's introduction to Dalma came late, only after his retirement from service. I accompanied him on his first trip to Dalma around 1977, a cherished memory. There I was, a rank outsider, showing a former Chief Conservator around what was once his own domain. I was not with him, however, during his near-fatal encounter with Gabbar Singh.

I think it was some time around March 1979. He was being driven down to Bijlighati, one of his favourite water holes, in a department jeep. Going past the first of the man-made reservoirs known as Barabandh, as he was driving down the twisting forest road, he saw a lone tusker in the water. The light was fine, and it was too good an opportunity to miss. He got off the jeep, and accompanied by the local forest range officer took his place on the raised rim of the reservoir, and started clicking away using a long lens. After a few shots, the slight metallic sounds of the camera's shutter disturbed the animal, and it slowly turned round to face the direction of the sound. It was then that the range officer recognised Gabbar Singh by the diagnostic broken tip of his right tusk, a scar of honour probably collected during a slight difference of opinion with a fellow-*mastan* of the forest.

The ranger, a grassroots forester, was well aware of Gabbar Singh's penchant for mischief, and in agitated whispers urged an immediate retreat. Shahi Sahib, on the other hand, had digested his Douglas-Hamilton well and was very hot on the idea of 'mock charge'. In fact, only a few months before while we were together in the Rajabhatkhowa forest rest house in Buxa, this was our recurring topic of animated dispute. My point was that the only way one could tell a mock charge from a real one was from the eventual outcome. A man killed? OK, it was for real. The man escaped: Ha! Ha! Obviously, a mock charge. Little had I realised then that the theory would be put to test so soon.

To come back to Dalma, Mr Shahi ignored the advice of the range officer and went on clicking his camera—after all, the light was so good, and the setting near perfect. The tusker took a few steps forward whereupon Shahi sahib calmly took off his tele-lens and changed back to normal—to get more of the background, as he genially explained to me later. Then, engrossed in composing his frames, he cleanly forgot that instead of a tele, he had a normal lens on. The elephant looked as large in the viewfinder as before. Plenty of distance, no need to worry, the jeep was only about thirty metres away. Then the tusker came forward in quick strides. Looking up from his camera, Shahi sahib discovered that the assumed distance had suddenly decreased by three-quarter, and the fellow was only a matter of a few feet away. Pulled up to his feet by the range officer, he started running down the slope towards the jeep. He just looked back once and saw that the tusker had crested the rim of the dyke. Then, he slipped and fell down, camera and all, and blacked out. The tusker came on. The range officer had the courage not to abandon his ex-chief. He stood by Shahi sahib and started shouting and waving the white towel he was carrying on his shoulder. This made Gabbar Singh stop momentarily. He managed to pull up a groggy Shahi sahib to his feet and both started running, followed by the tusker. Shahi sahib fell down once again near the jeep, but the sudden sound of the diesel engine of the jeep starting halted Gabbar Singh, and Shahi sahib lived to comment on the miracle of his camera having escaped with only a slight damage, the only miracle he ever discerned in the whole business. Somehow, he was distinctly less enthusiastic about 'mock charges' then on.

Next April saw us in a family group in Dalma. Dalma in late March–early April is all flowers and the bright green of new shal leaves. Kanchan of several colours, palash, the yellow silk-cotton tree (*galgali* as it is called locally) and shrubs of every kind all burst into flower together at this time of the year. The breeze is cool in the evenings. The lights of Jamshedpur from the TISCO bungalow on top of Dalma look like a carpet glowing with colour. The spirit of *joie de vivre* is everywhere.

On reaching Dalma we learnt that Gabbar Singh was still around, doing his very best to live up to his *mastan* image.

That was a year of drought. The man-made reservoirs on top of Dalma were much used by the fifty-odd elephants which annually retreat to the top of the Dalma Hills to spend their summer, very Raj-like. One of my objectives was to assess the status of the water-holes, some recently dug by the forest department to ease the stress of the drought on elephants. Things had advanced a lot since my first visit to Dalma around 1974 or so. The major water-holes now had concrete viewing boxes from where visitors could observe and photograph in safety, elephants coming to the water. We chose the Majhela Bandh pillbox—actually a small square room of concrete—as our viewing point. Parking the jeep on the forest road, we climbed down a gentle slope to the box-like structure overlooking the waterhole. The snag was that the structure was suffocatingly hot on an April afternoon. Apparently, this inconvenience had struck some earlier visitors as well, for we found a rickety ladder made of thin shal poles, struts tied with strips of bark, propped against its side. We, therefore, decided to perch ourselves atop the pillbox instead of venturing within.

It was nearing four in the afternoon when we were all comfortably settled on the roof—I with my cameras, my friend with a copy of Chomsky, of all authors, and the others, including three children. I was convinced that it would be a futile vigil; for, with a copy of Chomsky around, no self-respecting elephant could be expected to venture near us. Then, we sat soaking in the ambience of the forest, the sound of dry leaves clattering down, the busy struttings of cattle egrets in the lush green grassy patches around the waterhole, the twitter of birds, the antics of a dragonfly on a dry twig overhead. Shutting his disciplined mind to all these inconsequential frivolities, my friend was immersed in his Chomsky, the picture of a raving intellectual lacking only the regulation straws in his hair.

Suddenly, there was a flutter among the egrets, a branch broke noisily, and out of nowhere appeared Gabbar Singh on the edge of the water, his identity clearly marked by the right tusk broken at the tip. He plunged straight into the water and with all the enjoyment of a consummate voluptuary, started his bath. All elephants delight in water, and Gabbar Singh was no exception. Gabbar Singh was in musth as could be seen from the swollen temples and the tell-tale black mark of the oily discharge from the temples. We were happy with our cameras, safe on top of the viewing box, the jeep reassuringly close by. The children were excited, the ladies agog and even my friend condescended to put away his Chomsky for a while in honour of the visitor. The glorious afternoon clothed in new leaves and Gabbar Singh exuding musth and male vigour appeared to be made for each other. The frolic in the water went on with all manner of lusty squelches, gurgles, and swishes as well as whooshes. The elephant, besides being a noisy feeder, is also a noisy bather. He lay down in the water on one side, the tip of his trunk, snorkel-like, sticking out of the water, quivering slightly. Then he turned on his other side. The tip of the trunk daintily rubbed the temporal orifice. He sat on his haunches in the shallow pool and wriggled his bottom about, rubbing it against submerged rocks—as thorough a cleaning as the finickiest of elephant mums could wish. He did everything in his bath except sing. Gabbar Singh, at peace with himself and the world, was totally indifferent to our presence, the clicks of our cameras, the excited ohs and ahs, the breathless whispers, the hissed admonitions, all barely fifty feet away and none of which could have escaped his extraordinarily sharp hearing.

The minutes rushed past, the sun's rim dipped, the shadows strode out. We heard the trumpeting of a calf some distance away. The local tracker accompanying us whispered that a herd was also approaching the water, and that it was time to leave, as soon as there would be too many elephants about. As if to confirm the forecast, another shrill nasal trumpet rang out from a different direction. We had had our fill of thrills; it was definitely time to leave. I felt it was also time to show off my jungle wisdom and nonchalance. 'Nothing to it,' I said. 'We'll get to the jeep, but first let me shoo away the fellow,' and I clapped my hands wearing the casual, slightly superior smile of a man who has seen it all. Gabbar Singh completely ignored it; there was not even the slightest break in the steady rhythm of the flapping of his ears. I clapped again, and louder. No response once again. My superior smile was freezing into a silly grin. Another trumpet, this time closer by. Feeling this was no time for niceties of bush etiquette, I shouted at the damned animal, who acknowledged it with a momentarily cocked pair of ears and nothing more. It was getting dark rapidly.

With two ladies in elegantly-flowing saris in the party, along with three children of unbounded and irrepressible exuberance, and an insouciant Gabbar Singh barely fifty feet away, the jeep on the road up a rocky slope suddenly looked too far away. I shouted louder with the full power of a pair of lungs steeled by decades of lecturing. Gabbar Singh replied with a rude *brrr,* blown into the water with his submerged trunk. Then, I invited all present to join the shouting party which they did with admirable alacrity and gusto. It appeared to have some effect on the closing herd—for the next trumpet in which one could almost detect a note of indignation, was from further away—but none at all on Gabbar Singh. Short of chucking Chomsky and the available Chomskyites at him, we had tried all the known tricks in the game on Gabbar Singh, but with no effect whatsoever. An unconventional tactic was obviously called for. As is common knowledge, elephants do not like being abused. I took resort to this next in sheer desperation. I confess, my style was somewhat cramped by the presence of the ladies and, especially, the children, and there was little help from my friend, Chomsky being of scant use in such basic matters. Whatever the reason, Gabbar Singh eventually decided that he had finished with his bath, and moved out of the water to a dusty pan on the other side of our concrete perch, increasing his distance from the jeep to a healthy hundred metres. Then, he started dusting himself thoroughly, to the utter disgust of the ladies. Fancy dust and dirt, bucketfuls of them, after all that cashing and cleaning! A bad example to the children!

That was all the concession that Gabbar Singh ever made to our protests. There was now a possibility of an organised retreat. The driver was asked to run to the jeep, start the engine, and keep it running. If the *mastan* came for the jeep, he was to drive away at once leaving us to a night under the stars. The tusker took no notice of the jeep's noise. Then the party in batches of two started making it to the jeep. While a group of two ran up the slope to the jeep, the rest kept a watch on Gabbar Singh, keeping up a loud running commentary on his behaviour for the benefit of those on the ground. Thus, in slow and anxious stages, we all retreated to the jeep and drove away, leaving Gabbar Singh to his toilet in the dustpan, with a vague feeling that we had been put in our place.

The next day was given to an inspection of the outlying waterholes. The range officer who had accompanied Mr Shahi the previous year kindly came to Dalma Top in his jeep to take me around. As there was no point in dragging the rest of the party along, it was decided that they would be left again at Majhela Bandh. We would return before dark and pick them up. Lightning never strikes the same place twice, I argued, and the same should apply to Gabbar Singh. As things turned out, I was right; what I had not noted, however, was that the adage did not apply to persons.

Depositing them on the familiar rooftop in the care of the dragonflies, egrets, cicadas, and barbets, we proceeded in the range officer's jeep towards the waterholes on the northern face of Dalma. There is a ring road sort of jeepable track which takes one right round Dalma along the West Bengal face of the hill, cutting back through the range at one stage and emerging near Dimna on the other side, close to Jamshedpur. We were taking a 'short cut' from Majhela Bandh to this skirting road when suddenly one of the tribal trackers we had with us said, '*Haathi*'. We stopped at once. There was certainly an elephant in dense cover on the right side of the road, standing at right angles to the road. Try as we might, we just could not make out if the animal was facing the road or facing away from it, and, most important, if it was our old friend Gabbar Singh himself. One did not want to take unnecessary chances with Singh*ji*. Ten minutes or more went like this; the animal standing absolutely still, no flapping of ears visible, always a bad sign that; and we no wiser. As this 'short cut' would save us quite a few miles and we did not have much time to complete our round, we hesitated to turn back; instead, we decided to have a close look on foot, keeping the jeep's engine running as a distraction for the animal. One tracker and I got off the jeep and tiptoed forward, hugging the edge of the road and the fringing bushes. It must have been a very funny sight, but somehow no one actually laughed. I looked back once or twice at the jeep, only to see a couple of grim faces behind the windscreen, and the completely blank face of the other tracker peeping out from the back. After advancing about twenty metres like this, the full outline of the animal emerged; and, low and behold, it was none other than G.S. himself, and facing the road to boot. The process of tiptoeing back to the jeep was considerably quicker; the last stretch, let me confess, becoming something of an undignified rush. There was now no choice. Our 'short cut' had been cut short by the big bully. It would have to be the longer route now.

Completing our inspection of the waterholes, we started retracing our way to Majhela Bandh. It was nearly five o'clock—enough time before dark to pick up our party. But Gabbar Singh meanwhile had had other ideas. Negotiating a sharp turn on that hilly forest road we suddenly saw him coming on straight at a clipping pace along the road with the purposeful air of one having an urgent appointment somewhere. He stopped seeing the jeep, and we gladly reciprocated the gesture. I could not help observing bitterly that it seemed one could not move a foot in this blighted Dalma without tripping over this bully. I was developing a definite feeling of being persecuted.

However, a little thing like a jeepload of people was not going to hold up for long a *mastan* like Gabbar Singh. Sure enough, after a few seconds he was on the move again, coming straight towards us. The right of way he obviously considered was his, come to think of it, strictly speaking, so it was too. We promptly started reversing; there was simply no space to turn the vehicle around on that narrow, hilly, forest a road. This went on by fits and starts for nearly half a kilometre—a nerve-racking business on that kind of road. Every time the engine of the diesel jeep was revved up, the tusker halted; as soon as the engine fell back to normal, it started coming again. Reversing all the way, at last we reached a wider strip and could turn the jeep around with some effort, the tusker closing in every second. With the jeep turned round, we were now in a position to outrace it—one relief. After proceeding down the road for another 200 metres or so, the tusker following us steadily all the while, I asked the driver to stop the vehicle, keeping the engine running, of course, so that I could climb out of the front seat and take a steady snap from the ground of our relentless pursuer. As soon as I was out of the vehicle and standing on the road, exposing my separate identity, the tusker stopped in its tracks and fanned out its ears—a sight, and a sign that never fail to quicken the pulse of an elephant fancier. It was about fifty metres away. I focused my camera and clicked the shutter. The instantaneous reaction to the metallic click was a headlong change. The massive head slightly cocked to one side and kept low, the trunk curled in, one piggy eye keeping me fixed in sight, Gabbar Singh came for me like a madly speeding killer Kolkata minibus. As if on a spring, I turned towards the jeep, but by then the driver had started to speed away. I somehow managed to fling myself into the jeep. Within seconds, at least 500 metres separated us from that great big hulk of mischief. After our previous evening's experience, it was as if Gabbar Singh was teaching us, the tyros, a lesson in how to shoo away undesirable elements. Craning our necks back, we could see the fellow no more. We stopped again. Time now for a decision. If we wanted to avoid that road—Gabbar Singh now disputing our right of way—we would have to circle down all the way to Dimna, then take the Jamshedpur–Ranchi highway, and come up the hill from the other side. If we did that, it would be at least eight or so in the evening before we could hope to reach our party on the waterhole. While they would be perfectly safe on the concrete platform where we had left them, they were unlikely to savour the hours of waiting in total darkness without any food or even a torch, and not knowing what had happened to us. Discretion suggested the longer Jamshedpur–Ranchi route; but there was also the nagging suspicion that one would never hear the last of it and that the story of how old D.K. abandoned his friends and family in the forest of the night in vain pursuit of idle pleasures would be dug up from time to time to make irrelevant points at inconvenient moments. One has to keep one's cool in such crises, and I was determined to keep mine. It was a matter of choice, the very stuff of Greek Tragedy. Firm in my resolve to avoid any error of judgement, I decided to give the old route another try. But first we had to find out what Singh*ji* was up to just then. We again turned the vehicle around, or to be precise, persuaded a very reluctant driver to do so, and proceeded towards the spot where we had been seen off by Gabbar Singh. There was no sign of him, which did not mean anything. Was he again up to his usual prank of waiting for us in dense cover by the wayside in gleeful anticipation? Knowing by now some of his ways, it was not only possible but also very probable. The only thing was to find out the ground situation on foot. The tiptoeing act was put on again—only this time I chose to opt out of the cast, pleading a bruised knee sustained in the course of jumping into the jeep.

Everybody was sympathetic, as they could see that I had not been built by Nature for such stunts as taking flying leaps into fast-moving jeeps. Our two trackers silently went forward for about a hundred metres, one of them with his head down looking for spoor on the dust road, we tensely watching their every movement. They abruptly pulled up at a spot, crouched down, moved to the side of the road where the ground sloped down towards West Bengal, watched the side of the road intently for a while, and then came back to the jeep in hurried but silent steps. Yes, Gabbar Singh was there all right, but not close to the road. He was standing under a mango tree some fifty metres down the slope. This was good enough to race past him even if he decided to come for the jeep once again. The plan worked. We were back in Majhela Bandh in time.

I never saw Gabbar Singh again. A few years later when I was back in Dalma, they said Gabbar Singh had been shot in West Bengal as a rogue; but I could never actually relate him to any particular rogue elephant shot in southwest Bengal. Maybe, Gabbar Singhs do not die; they just fade away.

Why was Gabbar Singh so aggressive? Apart from his musth in the present case, the answer I think lay in his half-broken right tusk exposing the nerve cavity. The entire inside of the remaining part of the tusk, the bone socket of which extends into the skull almost up to the eyes, must have become infected, and the animal must have been in agony all the time. Just think of what a bad toothache does to one's temper, and judging by the size of his infected tooth, Gabbar Singh's must have been the 'mother of all toothaches'. I have known such animals to turn rogues. Once such an animal had to be destroyed. During the inspection of the carcass it was discovered that the entire tusk cavity was chock-full of maggots. And, looking back, if we resented bumping into him every time we moved out in Dalma, he on his part had all the reason to object to our popping up everywhere in his path. At least, we did not have the toothache; Gabbar Singh did. Poor, poor, Gabbar Singh!

Extracted from *A Trunk Full of Tales: Seventy Years with the Indian Elephant*, Permanent Black, 2006

# Winds of Change

*JOANNA VAN GRUISEN*

*Joanna Van Gruisen is a wildlife photographer, writer and conservationist. Her photographs and articles have been published in many magazines, books and newspapers in India and abroad. Her particular interests include the political ecology of conservation and bridging the gap between biological and social sciences. Her passion for the Himalayan region, which she describes as 'amongst the most endangered environments of the world', was initially kindled by the writings of nineteenth-century explorers but took serious root in 1981 when she was working on a wildlife film in Jammu and Kashmir.*

*Her article on the wildlife of Kashmir and the once-isolated region of Ladakh reflects her love for the Himalayas and her abiding concern whether the fragile ecology and culture of this cold desert will survive the impact of modern times. Seeing the area as a 'microcosm' of the planet, she reminds us that there is an essential interrelationship between conservation and development and that ultimately what is at stake is the survival of the human species.*

My first stay in an Indian jungle was, accidentally, in an area most reminiscent of my country of birth. The Dachigam National Park in Kashmir was home for fourteen months and its distinctive and beautiful seasonal changes were familiar. They were more in accordance with my British body rhythms than the hot and dry/hot and wet division of the climate in Sri Lanka where I had been residing for the previous few years. Maybe, this was one of the roots of my passion for the mountains, especially the Himalayan region of north-west India.

Dachigam consists of a stunningly lovely series of interlocking valleys spread over only 140 sq km but ranging from 1,800 metres to 4,400 metres; the park and its surrounds are the only place in the world where the highly endangered Hangul or Kashmir stag, a species of red deer, is found. At the time of my stay, nearly thirty years ago and in the quiet before the political turmoil, there were estimated to be around 400 hangul and they were increasing. In 2008, they are at a critical juncture of possible extinction as the latest census report reveals only 160 animals and a seriously low recruitment rate. However, not all the denizens of this somewhat beleaguered park have fared so badly in the intervening years: though no actual scientific studies to prove so, it would seem that there is reasonable evidence to believe that the leopard numbers have increased and the Himalayan black bear population is as good or perhaps even better than it was when I first visited.

I have a special soft spot for bears—these endearing but potentially dangerous to humans, animals. This is due to enjoying a very close relationship with an orphaned cub that we helped raise during the year we lived in Dachigam. He was a delightful creature and rarely showed any aggression in spite of growing from a cuddly, football-tummy-ed baby to an omnivore, taller and heavier than my not-small size. His substantial bulk was particularly brought home to me one day when, as a fully-grown adult, he enveloped me in a bear hug that was quite literally inescapable—until someone came by and enticed him away with food! Throughout our time together, he only became a bit grumpy and unpredictable after eating meat! But his diet was mainly vegetarian so these were rare occasions. My affection for bears has not even been diminished by a too close encounter with an extremely cantankerous wild adult female in the forests of Dachigam many years later (maybe, she had breakfasted on venison!). I strongly suspect that the only reason I am alive and in the unmutilated shape I am, is thanks to my very brave companion of the time—Abdul Rehman Mir, a wildlife guard from the nearby Harwan village. Instead of running away to save his own life when the bear charged, he heroically stepped back towards me and thereby bore the full attack. The bear inflicted a few deep and painful bites and scratches, which, fortunately, just managed to miss all vital points. Having thus knocked him to the ground, she seemed content and scampered away. We never could figure why she felt the need to charge; we were on different paths and no threat and Rehman had met her at closer quarters on many previous occasions with no such result. Strange, but then this is why the epithet of 'unpredictable' is so often used in connection with bears!

Dachigam was also where the seed was sown for another long-term affair of the heart. It was there that we met Sir Robert Ffolkes, then head of Save the Children Fund in Ladakh, whose conversation totally whetted my appetite for those even higher lands. His story of a village archery contest in a remote village of the trans-Himalayas and of the snow leopard pair that were spotted on a ridge overlooking the event engendered an image impossible to resist. It was only a matter of time before I found my way to the trans-Himalayan region and having found it, returned and returned—and return. The snow leopard was the first lure but soon the magnet became the entirety of the environment and people.

The trans-Himalayas is an extensive area of more than two and a half million sq kms: a small percentage of this—around 180,200 sq kms—lies in Jammu and Kashmir and in fact constitutes 80 percent of the state's land area. A further 6,000 sq kms lie in Himachal Pradesh and much smaller patches in Sikkim and Uttarakhand. The trans-Himalayas is the vast mountainous region that lies beyond, and in the rain shadow of the main Himalayan range. It is a fascinating and fragile area of enormous importance. Three of our major rivers—the Indus, the Chenab and the Sutlej—have their main catchment areas in the trans-Himalayas, this notwithstanding the fact that it is a high altitude desert region of very low precipitation, most of which falls in the form of snow. Also, the area and its glaciers are critical to millions in the Indian subcontinent; and in today's world of galloping climate change and glacier melt, it is a region that demands serious and focussed attention. The fast disappearing glaciers are not only severely effecting the sparse population dependent on their water in the immediate vicinity, but as drying up 'water towers' of the subcontinent, this will have major impacts far beyond.

Many visitors to the trans-Himalayan regions, while struck by the immensity and drama of the landscapes, are unaware of the rich biodiversity that has adapted to survive here. More often than not, such areas are referred to as 'barren wastelands': how incorrect such labels are! In reality it is a region of high diversity in both flora and fauna, although it is true that the extremities of the environment mean that densities are likely to be low; the animals, therefore, need relatively larger areas to maintain viable populations. The extremes, the intense cold and aridity, the short summer growth periods and low productivity make the area very precarious and easily susceptible to being damaged.

The peoples who settled in these areas also had to adapt to the somewhat hostile environment and, over the centuries, developed ways of living that were appropriate for the climate and surroundings, managing to survive in settlements as high as 4,500 metres above sea-level. It was a tough existence and did not encourage dense population growth! We also habitually refer to the area as being 'remote', which, of course, from an elsewhere-in-India perspective it is. But Ladakh is geographically fairly central to the Inner Asian landmass and has historically been on the trade and cultural exchange map long before roads from the south reached. Culturally, Ladakh looked north, east and west more than south and so with its natural history: the species to be found here fall in the Paleartic, Mediterranean and Chinese groups. Apart from three members of the cat family, four canids and nine ungulates, there are a host of smaller mammals, around 225 bird species and perhaps fourteen reptiles; many of these are listed in Schedule I of the Wildlife (Protection) Act and several have interesting adaptations, enabling survival in the extreme environment of the area. Not bad for a 'barren wasteland'!

The snow leopard is, of course, one of the most charismatic animals to be found here; it is both a flagship and an umbrella species. It also has a reputation of being one of the most elusive of creatures: in large part due to magnificent camouflage which is manifested not only in its pelage of blending-colours, broken with distracting rosettes, but also in the way it can move. This was very much brought home to us one particular day when half a dozen eagle-eyed scientists, wildlife managers and naturalists (myself included) were scanning an open slope, with binoculars and telescope, trying to locate a full-grown radio-collared male. We knew he was there, lying up on a rocky patch. And in the time that we longingly examined every bump and stone and bit of vegetation across the slope hoping that they would metamorphise into a living cat, in front of our eyes he traversed that very hillside and went over the ridge without any of us picking up his movement! All this we confirmed later from the indirect signs. We have had several such encounters, or non-encounters, and have learnt how beautifully they can just melt away: now you see me, now you don't!

But I am one of the very fortunate who has watched snow leopards in the wild; my very first sighting was of three together—a mother and two large cubs. But I nearly missed them too, thanks this time to the exigencies of the bureaucracy! The visa authorities discovered they needed my urgent presence in Delhi and I received the message while in a remote, one-house village. It was a day's walk from Leh and the airport where I could catch the flight out (the only way to leave Ladakh in the winter when snow blocks the high road passes). I was several months into a project to film Ladakh's wildlife, especially the snow leopard. We had become immensely fit as we traversed many mountains and valleys following the advice of local friends and experts in our search for the snow leopard; but we had yet to lay eyes on our dream. We had begun concentrating in an area suggested by the wonderful local Range Officer, (the now tragically late) Chering Norbu. These were also the valleys chosen by a Wildlife Institute of India scientist, Raghu Chundawat, for his Ph.D. study. With Raghu and his research assistants also moving in the area, the chance of finding snow leopards was increased. Also as part of his project, he was hoping to collar some animals and we wanted to film the event. Norbu, Raghu and I had been staying in the village, exploring the valley and watching one of the leopards' major prey species, the bharal or napo. (This is also known as the blue sheep but as it is neither terribly blue nor exactly a sheep, I prefer not to use the term).

Most reluctantly, I had temporarily packed my bags for the enforced visit to Delhi. Norbu sahib was accompanying me to Leh, so we set off behind the small horses carrying our baggage. A half hour or more along the way, we heard Raghu's assistant calling and turned to see him gesticulating at us as he hurried to catch up. He carried a vague message about Raghu seeing a snow leopard. I had heard such a tale too often to immediately turn and run back (all our months' exploration to date had been following such reports: it was here just now, just yesterday, just last week. . . .) But it was tantalising, so we alerted the horseman to stop our small caravan and waited for more details. It seemed there was a kill. This sounded too promising, so burying anxieties about my civic duties, we turned and hurried back. That night, freezing in a small cloth hide, I saw my first snow leopard; indeed my first three snow leopards; in the light of the moon. Magic! I stayed an extra day and even managed to get a little daylight footage but dared not delay longer. I must have been crazy, giving up three snow leopards just to renew a visa!

Fortunately however, there were a few other occasions, though none with quite that potential. I never saw more than one at a time after that and the only event that rivalled it for excitement was when I witnessed a snow leopard expropriate a kill from four wild dogs. It just left them standing, frustrated but too uncertain to approach, as it took their prey towards the cliffs. It was an interesting episode, especially as in the plains of India such thefts occur more often the other way around—the dhole (wild dog) pack taking the kills from the tiger or leopard. Seeing the wild dog in Ladakh was as thrilling as viewing the snow leopard. This is the same animal of the plains but its long coat, protection against the trans-Himalayan cold, gives it quite a different appearance, almost cuddly, rather than the lean-mean-eating-machine look of the ones in the Peninsula forests. It was of added interest as although the phara, as it is called there, was well-known to the local community, its presence then (in the late 1980s) had apparently not been confirmed to the satisfaction of the outside scientific world for some time.

This happened twenty years ago . . . but it seems another era. Ladakh was first wafted by winds of the 'modernised' world after Independence, when Ladakh's future was linked to India, along with Kashmir's. As a strategic border area, there has been significant Indian army presence in the region. In 1974, it opened for tourism; since then, outside visitors have increased from a few hundred to over 22,000 annually. But the modern winds took time to affect Ladakh. In 1981, a Ladakhi author could write: 'The fact is that Ladakh has not undergone any severe or radical change as of today.' (*Ladakh, Between Earth and Sky*, Siddiq Wahid, 1981.) He could describe a way of life that had changed little over the centuries. This does not hold so true today. Those insidious winds carry seeds strong enough to threaten the fabric of this valuable culture and have brought destructive elements inappropriate for this fragile ecosystem. There are lessons here for us all: what is happening in Ladakh is a microcosm in time and area of issues affecting the whole planet. Endangered wildlife is but the first to go: we would do well to remember that they developed in the same world as us and if we make it untenable for them, it will become so for humans.

One of the most delicately balanced parts of the world is the Tibetan plateau; eastern Ladakh encompasses the beginning of this plateau, one that to me is one of the most breathtakingly beautiful and fascinating regions in the world. It is a vast high altitude desert landscape of rolling mountains, white peaks, azure blue lakes and high flat valleys (over 4,500 metres). As elsewhere in Ladakh, the land appears vast and empty: but a closer look reveals an amazing variety of living creatures, from burrowing mouse hare to the striking kiang, from scurrying lizards to graceful skeins of geese, the diminutive vole to the magnificently large-horned Tibetan argali sheep and each has its own way of surviving the harsh conditions.

The region is too high for agriculture but humans have managed to make their home here too. Nature is powerful and unforgiving and lives have been adapted to adjust to her whims. The people here live a nomadic life; they raise sheep, goats and yaks and survive largely on the products of their livestock. The yaks provide strong hair that is woven and sewn to provide their tented accommodation. The goats provide milk and are the key to the Changpas' wealth. In these high cold mountains, they grow fine protective underwool and this is collected and spun to create the fine and beautiful pashmina shawls for which Kashmir is famous. The Changpas' lives revolve around care of their livestock, movements have been carefully developed over the centuries, to maximise production in a delicate ecosystem. The sparse vegetation has to be grazed in rotation and the delicate balance of nature's sustainability maintained. Their success in surviving over the centuries is testament to their wisdom and abilities; they have moulded their lives to the limitations of the extremes within which they live; it is a hard life and their Buddhist faith both aids and complements the strenuous existence.

Thus, it is a rare area where humans and wildlife live in a certain harmony. Each creature plays its role in maintenance of the ecosystem and has evolved within an intricate high altitude community. People and their livestock have become a part of this, accepting the wild animals as an element of their challenging environment. Live and let live—the wildlife and people adjust to each other.

When people and livestock move to other valleys from their winter quarters by the lake, the wild birds move in to breed: geese, ducks, grebes, gulls and waders, even the rare black-necked crane. The Himalayan marmots appear from hibernation as the vegetation sprouts, and feed assiduously to accumulate enough fat for their next winter sleep. Little owls fly through glassless windows to nest in the abandoned homes and mouse hare scamper over the rock walls. In August, the wild ass mares drop their foals and move down to the valley floors, taking advantage of the richer vegetation around the lakes. Come late summer and the kiang stallions fight for their leks (small defended territorial patches) ready for the early autumn drama of the rutting season. When the winter snows begin, the birds fly to warmer climes as the lakes freeze over and the Changpas return. The kiang move onto the slopes and to other pastures as the people and livestock reclaim the valley grassland.

But there is one creature that, instead of avoiding the human community, actively seeks them out and is more often found around the Changpa camps than elsewhere. This predator finds the domestic livestock an easy prey option and especially in winter, when the marmots retire, takes a toll on the local people's capital. The Tibetan wolf, possibly the oldest lineage of this canid family, is a wily predator of these high altitude plains and its interaction with the people mirrors that of humans and predators since the domestication of animals.

But these old ways are passing: international winds of change now blow through this ancient equilibrium: some beneficial, others more destructive. Bottled cooking gas replaces fires of dung and scrub vegetation; SUVs replace the traditional horses; Changpa children move to towns for education, the induction to a new life, new work options. Tourists and trekkers bring new strains: flush toilets, plastics, roads, rubbish. The scales rock; can a new balance be found? The past may not be perfection but the present appears very imperfect. Can modern learning appreciate the wisdom of centuries? Can the wildlife and nomadic culture of this previously so-secluded region, survive the pull into a universalised world? Can we globalised individuals appreciate the lessons of a simpler culture?

# The Leopard

*RUSKIN BOND*

*He is a man of the mountains, and a sculptor of words who has enthralled readers from the age of seven to seventy. Ruskin Bond writes stories, poetry, and essays. He writes of trees and train journeys, of lost loves and funerals, of flowers and tigers, of ghosts and cricket, and so much more, in a language that charms the reader with its simplicity. Bond has a rare sense of humour, and a sense of melancholy, that ensures that the stories stay with you long after you have put the book down. The writer lives in Landour, and wrote his first novel* The Room on the Roof *when he was 17. It has a biological flavour—like most of his writing. He has subsequently authored many collections like* Night Train at Deoli, Delhi is Not Far, A Season of Ghosts; *among others. Bond has won the Sahitya Academy Award and has also been conferred a Padma Shri. A work of fiction,* The Leopard *brings out in an unassuming manner the beauty of the beast, and the ruthlessness of man. Bond wishes that we,* Homo sapiens *be sensitive towards the leopard, and that it will continue to roam the forests and hills forever. But is this hope in vain. . . . ?*

I first saw the leopard when I was crossing the small stream at the bottom of the hill. The ravine was so deep there that for most of the day it remained in shadow. This encouraged many birds and animals to emerge from cover even during the hours of daylight. Few people ever passed that way: only milkmen and charcoal-burners from the surrounding villages. As a result, the ravine had become a little haven of wild life, one of the few natural sanctuaries left in the area.

Nearly every morning, and sometimes during the day, I heard the cry of the barking-deer. In the evening, walking through the forest, I disturbed parties of kaleej pheasant, who went gliding down the ravine on open, motionless wings. I saw pine-martens and a handsome red fox. I recognised the footprints of a bear.

As I had not come to take anything from the jungle, the birds and animals soon 'grew accustomed to my face,' as Mr Higgins would say. More likely, they recognised my footfalls. My approach did not disturb them. A Spotted Forktail, which at first used to fly away, now remained perched on a boulder in the middle of the stream while I got across by means of other boulders only a few yards away. Its mellow call followed me up the hillside.

The langurs in the oak and rhododendron trees, who would at first go leaping through the branches at my approach, now watched me with some curiosity as they munched the tender green shoots of the oak. But one evening, as I passed, I heard them chattering with excitement; and I knew I was not the cause of the disturbance.

As I crossed the stream and began climbing the hill, the grunting and chattering increased, as though the langurs were trying to warn me of some hidden danger. I looked up, and saw a great orange-gold leopard, sleek and spotted, poised on a rock about twenty feet away from me. The leopard looked at me once, briefly and with an air of disdain, and then sprang into a dense thicket, making absolutely no sound as he melted into the shadows.

I had disturbed the leopard in his quest for food. But a little later I heard the quickening cry of a barking-deer as it fled through the forest.

After that encounter I did not see the leopard again although I was often made aware of his presence by certain movements.

Sometimes I thought I was being followed; and once, when I was late getting home and darkness closed in on the forest I saw two bright eyes staring at me from a thicket. I stood still my heart thudding against my ribs. Then the eyes danced away and I realised that they were only fireflies.

One evening, near the stream, I found the remains of barking-deer, which had only been partly eaten. I wondered why the leopard had not hidden the remains of his meal, and decided that he had been disturbed while eating. Climbing the hill, I met a party of shikaris resting beneath the pine trees. They asked me if I had seen a leopard. I said I had not. They said they knew there was a leopard in the forest. Leopard-skins were selling in Delhi at a thousand rupees each, they told me; I walked on.

But the hunters had seen the carcass of the deer, and they had seen the leopard's pug-marks, and they had kept coming to the forest. Almost every evening I heard their guns banging away.

'There's leopard about,' they always told me. 'You should carry a gun.'

'I don't have one,' I said.

The birds were seldom to be seen, and even the langurs had moved on. The red fox did not show itself; and the pine-martens, who had become quite bold, now dashed into hiding at my approach. The smell of one human is like the smell of any other.

And then, of course, the inevitable happened.

The men were coming up the hill, shouting and singing. They had a long bamboo pole across their shoulders, and slung from the pole, feet up, head down, was the lifeless body of the leopard. He had been shot in the neck and in the head.

'We told you there was a leopard!' they shouted, in great good humour. 'Isn't he a fine specimen?'

'He was a fine leopard,' I said.

I walked home through the silent forest. It was very silent, almost as though the birds and animals knew that their trust had been violated.

'And God gave Man dominion over the fish of the sea and over the fowl of the air, and over the cattle, and over all the earth, and over every creeping thing that creepeth upon the earth. . . .'

For a leopard-skin coat, value one thousand rupees.

First published in *The Illustrated Weekly of India*, 1972

# Red Cancer Green Quarry

*PRERNA SINGH BINDRA*

*I had some misgivings about this article finding place in the anthology, for in a sense the story is strictly reportage. Yet, maybe it is warranted, as a reality check of sorts. One of the major problems confronting our country today is naxal insurgency. The present Prime Minister, Dr Manmohan Singh has described it as 'the biggest threat to internal security.' There is a lot of complexity attached to this issue, but that is beyond the scope of this book. What is of concern is that the base of left-wing extremism (naxalism) is our forests. That is where the naxals live, train, and operate from. Our forests are, in other words, nursing terror. My travels into forests across the country showed that many prime tiger habitats have become the citadel of naxals. What were once verdant jungles are now sanctuaries for left-wing extremists, and not for wild creatures.*

*Admittedly, there is no documentation to establish that the naxals are endangering our wildlife, and the issue is open to debate. Indeed, there are some indications quite to the contrary. A recent report says that forest cover has increased, very marginally, in naxal-affected areas. On the other hand, we know they are given 'protection money' by timber contractors. In some areas, they are instigating the clearing of forests to cultivate marijuana, or cannabis. Adding to the complexity is the fact that local goons and mafia have taken advantage of the situation and are operating under the guise of naxals.*

*This article is my attempt to report, from ground zero, the parks ravaged by insurgency.*

I wish I had met Mahindra, the resident tusker of Simlipal Tiger Reserve (Orissa), in better times. He is known for his arrogance and nasty temper, and is considered a one 'man' anti-poaching squad. His most recent exploit was to chase down a gang of timber smugglers and destroy the tools of their trade—axes, bikes and guns—with one well-aimed kick.

I watched him now, a shadow of his former cocky self. He limped painfully, eyed his food with indifference and shuffled listlessly as a mahout poured antibiotics on his wounds. Mahindra is a victim of the Naxal attack on Simlipal in March 2009. He was shot—nine bullets pumped into his body—and left to die.

He survived, having received timely assistance. But will Simlipal?

Doubtful. It's no one's child; abandoned by forest officials and discounted by the state government when it was under siege by extremists for over a week—its worst crisis.

**'Simlipal ravaged. Lost to Naxals'** was the sms that woke me at dawn on 29 March 2009. The Naxals had struck the Tiger Reserve the night before. Their very first attack was the crippling one, destroying the main wireless tower at Meghasani, Similipal's highest peak, thereby cutting off communications of both the forest guard and the police, in the region. The synchronised first wave of attacks lasted just over fourteen hours (though the siege itself continued for another week). Forest chowkis, range offices and vehicles were burnt, rest houses were pillaged, rangers and forest guards were tied up and beaten, tourists were looted and held hostage. The attacks occurred across the 2,750 sq km reserve, but were mainly concentrated at its most vulnerable points—Chahala, Upper Barhakamuda, Devasthali, Gudgudiya, Patbil, Jenabil, and Joranda, all within the critical core area where tigers, and other wildlife are concentrated.

Through that first series of coordinated attacks, Simlipal was effectively rendered unprotected. The forest department fled the field, having 'surrendered within twenty-four hours', in the words of the then director of the park. There were just two remaining police groups posted in the buffer zones of the reserve.

Simlipal Tiger Reserve was, and continued to be, open for loot.

## The Door to Desolation

'At your own risk,' I was warned by officials when I expressed my desire to enter Simlipal. The Naxals may still be inside, they said; the locals were hostile (there is evidence that they were involved in the attack), there was the lurking risk of landmines, and yes, the roads and bridges could be blocked or blown up—no one could be sure about the situation inside the reserve.

The first hitch occurred even before we entered the Pithabata gate. A jeep stopped in front of us, almost ramming into our vehicle, just as we approached. The men inside were palpably drunk. And very palpably armed. 'It is better if you turn back,' they threatened in the local tongue; 'there are Naxals inside, and they don't welcome outsiders.'

We ignored the warning and entered the gate. The ranger seated at the one-room office at Pithabata was frightened, and with good reason. A week back, the Naxals had barged in, exploded a few country-made bombs, coerced and threatened the staff, and stuck posters proclaiming 'Death to Project Tiger'.

We drove on. The park wore a desolate air; there were a few traces of wildlife—a lone chowsingha (four-horned antelope), a few peafowl and very rarely, some elephant dung. There were, however, signs of devastation everywhere. I covered some vital areas—Nawana, where the range office was burnt down, Joranda, where the tents put up for tourists received the same treatment, before moving on towards Gudgudia, which is where the tusker was shot. Near Gudgudia, I halted at a village, Lanjhaghesra. The locals were unwelcoming and hostile. They denied any knowledge of the mayhem: 'We do not know anything. It happened at night. We were fast asleep after our drink of *hadiya*,' said Mata Alda, a villager. Police sources say that back in March, this same village was part of a huge gathering of a cluster of villagers here as a show of strength against the forest department. It is suspected that Naxal elements were also present.

The road to Chahala was blocked by a tree. We removed it, not without some difficulty. Chahala is in the heart of the reserve where the kings of Mayurbhanj once hunted . . . so fecund was the forest. In contemporary times, it served as a magnificent arena for the theatre of the wild—huge herds of cheetal, hundreds of sambar, groups of elephants, lone tuskers, all visiting the nearby salt lick for their daily dose of minerals. Predators came in pursuit of their prey, and leopard sightings were not uncommon. Tigers? Yes, one had just walked by weeks ago. . . .

But now, ten days since the attack, Chahala wore the look of a ghost 'town'.

There were no signs of life. The silence was eerie, and not a reflection of the peace that is the blessing of a forest. We took in the devastation—the range office had been gutted, the wireless system smashed, wildlife monitoring registers burnt to ash, bikes reduced to blackened skeletons, the rest house furniture and toilets demolished. On a wall there was a faded picture of a tiger, looking down (poignantly, I imagined) at his ravaged kingdom. 'Symbolic,' I thought, while getting ready to take a photograph, when a gunshot cut through the air.

Hunters!

I rushed out *(photograph forgotten)* to see a party of poachers, some six of them, maybe more, accompanied by dogs and armed with local weaponry, spears, *tangi* (axe), bows and arrows, and *charra*, the local gun. We gave chase but they were too fast and too familiar with the forest. My worst fears were realised—with the forest guards gone, poachers were having a field day at Simlipal.

I sent an SOS to the police to get forces into the critical area. They will, I was promised, when . . . we did not know.

Policing is anyway not the only answer to this multi-layered issue. The incident has revealed a clear and disturbing pattern, with implications that reach far beyond Simlipal. For starters, the attacks were clearly aimed to break the forest administration and 'free' the forest of any form of state control whatsoever. Foresters fled the field in terror; none dared return. Narhari Naik, a forester who had witnessed the carnage said they were warned—if they returned to their posts, they would pay with their lives.

The timing of the attack was another masterstroke—it was engineered on the eve of *akhand shikar*, a month-long annual ritual of the local tribals, wherein they go on a mass hunting spree armed with indigenous weapons, killing every animal in sight. The field was clear then, not just for *akhand shikar*, but for poachers who had been targeting Simlipal incessantly over the years. About eight to ten elephants are killed annually, though most deaths go unreported. Tigers and leopards are poached regularly. So much so, some even say that poachers have 'used' the Naxals, teaming up with them to drive away any semblance of control. The other possibility is that this is a masterstroke of the timber mafia to gain control of the forest. Given that huge poaching gangs rushed in after the attack, and went on a carnage killing rare, wild creatures, the theory can't be fully refuted.

I met the police officers later, those in charge here; they were old hands in working in 'red' country. Naxals, they explained, were encouraged by the tacit support of the forest dwellers and tribals, who have nurtured a sense of hostility vis-à-vis the forest department. The department is an impediment in their activities, be it ritual hunting or tree felling for fuel wood or commercial purposes. This resentment was exploited by the Naxals. Another factor was the sheer apathy of the forest department. The attack was a result of a meticulous plan, indicating Naxal presence in the park for a considerable period, though their presence went unnoticed—a tragic failure on the part of the forest department. Such warfare does not occur overnight, but sheer indifference ensured that things came to pass.

It is also evident that the Naxals are in cahoots with the timber and Sal mafia, and have the active or tacit support of some local politicians. The illicit trade of Sal leaf in Orissa is valued at an unbelievable Rs 1,000 crore annually, mainly sourced from Simlipal. About 150–200 trucks carry the booty out daily, and the Naxals certainly have a stake.

## Nurseries of Terror

What is happening in Simlipal is, of course, a microcosm of a pan-India phenomenon. Across India extremist forces are sheltering in forests and deriving their finances from the trade in forest produce and, to a certain extent, in wildlife derivatives like ivory, rhino horn, tiger skins, etc. Forests provide asylum and are indeed, the nurseries of Naxals. This is where they seek shelter, base their training schools, and plan their strikes.

Over 11 million hectares of forest area across India are under the control of extremist forces. Writes Bittu Sahgal, editor, *Sanctuary Asia*, '[From] Naxal groups in Andhra Pradesh, MP, Bihar, Chattisgarh, Jharkhand and Maharashtra to separatists in Assam's Karbi Anglong, have been linked with the illegal trade in timber, wildlife derivatives and narcotics over the past decade.'

Red terror has control of huge tracts of tiger country, and the menace is steadily growing. Nearly a third of our tiger reserves have been lost to Naxals. Tigers don't thrive where Naxals do—tiger density in Naxal-affected forests is a paltry 0.5 to 1.5 tigers per 100 sq km, by some estimates.

I have travelled to some of these places, where the 'reds' have made inroads, or overruled the greens—forests which are beyond our control, or are nurseries of terror.

Indravati in Chhattisgarh is perhaps the worst case scenario. Naxals call the shots here, and timber is fast being converted into cash by the Naxal-contractor-politician nexus. They have taken a heavy toll on forest staff, too; and the forest department has not dared enter Indravati for about a decade. One can only guess the state of affairs: How many tigers survive? Indeed, do any survive at all? The All India Tiger Estimation could not be conducted here, it was just too risky.

Let's move on to Palamu Tiger Reserve in Jharkhand, which was once verdant with khair trees. Khair is used to derive *katha*, the vital ingredient of paan and gutkha (a tobacco mixture).

Palamu is now almost emptied of khair; the tigers have all but vanished; only the Maoists flourish.

It is a well-established fact that the extremists were being financed by the *katha* mafia. Contractors paid huge amounts to Maoists as 'protection money' to carry out the felling [of khair trees]. So immense was the scale that the collector of the district recommended that all khair be felled to curb Naxal activity and crime.

I have been to Palamu and the horror continues to haunt me. Several rangers and guards had been killed, their heads chopped off, their bodies blown to bits by landmines. Forest offices and homes had been set afire, tusks stolen. More recently, the field director of Palamu was kidnapped by Maoists and given a list of demands—vehicles, fuel, etc. The underlying threat if the demands weren't met was apparent.

It must be noted here that the illicit trade in gutkha is huge, running into Rs 1,500 crore annually. Even the 'D Company' (i.e. an organised crime and terror outfit) has a stake in the gutkha pie, and acquires the raw material mainly from Kollegal and Chamrajnagar in Karnataka, and some pockets in Maharashtra from groups associated with Naxals.

Yet another paradise lost is Saranda, the beautiful 'land of seven hundred hills' in Jharkhand. It was the largest and the finest Sal forest in Asia and home to many elephants and tigers. It is now a graveyard. I visited it in mid-2005. I landed late at night, after bumping endlessly over what passed as roads—destroyed by Naxals to discourage connectivity. All that remained of the forest rest house where I was supposed to stay was its charred ruins. The ranger I turned to refused to open the door at that hour—his predecessor, had answered a knock on his door, and had been beheaded eight months back. No one accompanied me inside the forest; there were landmines, and just two weeks before my arrival a posse of security personnel had been blown to bits. In November 2008 the ranger had a lucky escape—his jeep was blown up, and it was pure chance that he wasn't in it.

In south Orissa in Kothgadh Wildlife Sanctuary, links between ivory trade and insurgency are well-established. The animal mortality rate is high, but these massacres rarely, if ever, make it onto official records. Forest officers fear to tread here and reporting such cases, says an officer previously posted at Kothgadh, 'is signing your death warrant'. Sunebada, a proposed tiger reserve in the state, has also been attacked repeatedly in the past few months. It is felt, though, that the naxal attack is a facade—it was the ganja mafia that struck to gain control of the illegal cultivation of ganja or cannabis that flourishes inside the sanctuary.

Naxals blew up tourist facilities in Nagarjunasagar – Srisailam Tiger Reserve in Andhra Pradesh in May 2006. Elsewhere in the state, in the forests of North Telengana, Maoist groups reportedly razed range offices and killed staff and a few tigers in what was essentially a show of power to the administration in the early 90s, particularly the forest department. The Naxals are gaining ground in other reserves as well – Valmiki in Bihar is already vulnerable, as is Sitanadi-Udanti, a newly declared tiger reserve in Chhattisgarh.

If we move to the northeast, the insurrection may have a different colour, but the separatist movement here is fuelled by the timber and poaching mafia as well. A forest officer in Karbi-Anglong, which serves as a vital corridor to the Kaziranga Tiger Reserve in Assam, informed me that the forest serves as a training ground for the Karbi Longri National Liberation Front, which is closely linked to ULFA, another militant group.

Though Manas Tiger Reserve in Assam is now on the mend, it is well-established that in the Bodo attack of 1992, the militants, and opportunistic poachers, had killed all the rhinos within a few years, massacred the tuskers, set the domestic elephants afire—yes, burnt them—and slaughtered the forest guards. A former poacher I met admitted to having personally killed eighty elephants and two tigers; that it financed the separatist struggle is left unsaid. (It is another—and very interesting—story that he, and the Bodos are now involved in conservation.)

Our forests are now sanctuaries for extremists, not tigers and other wildlife.

## A Soft State

Simlipal was a tragedy waiting to happen. Mayurbhanj district has long been a haven for Left-wing extremists, given its contiguity to Saranda. The police officer I met said that the Naxals are attempting to create a red corridor that connects Jharkhand with Keonjhar and Jajpur, where they have made significant inroads already.

It's unlikely that the problem will be curbed, given that the Maoists seem to enjoy the covert patronage of the current state government, the Biju Janata Dal (BJD). This is suggested by the fact that in the last decade, roughly the time the BJD government has been in power, the number of Naxal-affected districts in the state has grown from three to twenty.

And even if there is no tacit support, a soft state has clearly allowed extremism to flourish, and as long as our forests are left unprotected there is little hope of curbing the Naxal menace.

Take the case of Simlipal. The director admitted his helplessness. Understaffed and unequipped as they were, they had no choice but to surrender. At present there are only thirty-six guards, most nearing the age of retirement, to man the entire reserve of 2,750 sq. km. (This is largely true of most of our reserves, which work with fifty–seventy percent staff shortage.) As recruitments have been frozen for about thirty years, the average age of a forest guard is fifty! They are mostly unarmed—at best they have defunct weapons—and are underpaid—a woefully inadequate green army to counter armed insurgents, and protect our forests. Another point is that it need not always be the Naxals themselves, but the crime syndicate of poaching-timber mafia that follows in their wake, or may be operating with the blessings of the extremist forces.

The local forest department cannot get away with playing the victim though: They have failed to win the constituency of the forest dwellers and those living on the fringes of the reserve, leading to a sense of hostility that the Naxals have exploited. Moreover, corrupt practices that have traditionally 'allowed' timber smuggling to flourish have meant that the contractors now simply fill the coffers of the Naxals instead of the bureaucrats.

Successive governments have chosen to ignore this aspect of the red threat to our security. In our apathy, we have surrendered our wilds to extremist forces, allowed our sanctuaries to become nurseries of terror. It has been estimated that separatists and insurgents are earning over Rs 200 crore annually from the timber and wildlife trade. Securing our forests against these forces is essential to combat them effectively, as is addressing issues like rehabilitation of forest dwellers and livelihood options, to break their support to Naxals. The question is, will our government realise that in time?

P.S.: There is a footnote to the story that I must mention. Independent teams were appointed by central government to assess tiger reserves under naxal control. Consistent pressure by the media and conservationists saw the Ministry of Environment and Forests take special efforts and initiatives to nurture Simlipal back to health. A good management team has been put in place, rehabilitating villages from the core areas has been given priority, and there are efforts to employ a special 'Tiger Protection Force.'

Nagarjunasagar has also been largely freed from naxal control, thanks to efforts by the AP government, and reports indicate that the reserve has the potential to be our finest tiger habitat.

First published in '*M*' May 2009, and
*Tehelka*, Issue 16, 25 April 2009

# Our Wild Heritage—A Hope for the Future

*Kailash Sankhala*

*This may have been composed many years back, but the author possessed the gift of foresight and wisdom, ensuring a timelessness to his words that holds true even today.* Our Wild Heritage *not only gives a brief history of wildlife conservation—and destruction—in India, but also explains how with political will and determined leadership we succeeded (then) in our efforts to save the tiger from man. Kailash Sankhala, the first director of Project Tiger, is best known as India's 'Tiger Man', but few know that Sankhala battled, successfully for the establishment of India's first Marine National Park in Gujarat and the Desert National Park in Rajasthan.*

*Sankhala was a Padma Shri awardee and the first civil servant to get the Jawaharlal Nehru Fellowship. Books authored by him include* The Story of Indian Tiger, The Return of the Tiger, Gardens of God. *The following chapter, extracted from a collection of his writings:* Lest We Forget, *also highlights Sankhala's insights into the threats to our wild heritage, which continue to exist, if in a more exaggerated manner. If only we had heeded Sankhala's quiet wisdom, our natural history of current times would read differently, far from the tragedy of crisis that it is today.*

The real destruction of India's forests, the major habitat of its wildlife, began under the rule of the East India Company, about 250 years ago. Extraction of timber for ship building and railroad sleepers in the United Kingdom as well as in India by British companies was the principal cause. To meet the needs of the two World Wars, they justified the excessive felling of forests, as 'war fellings'. But the worst was yet to come—the confusion during our transition from a colony to an independent republic proved to be disastrous. The planned felling of forests was undertaken without any understanding of the functioning of forest eco-systems. A forest is a multifaceted, intricate living organism and balanced forestry entails a long-term sustainable management system. Low priorities, confused management and weak leadership are disastrous. In our forestry, we had all the handicaps.

Enthusiasm for plantations was at the cost of natural forests. To consider stands of monocultured rows of eucalyptus trees or impenetrable bushland of *Prosopis juliflora* as a forest—a living composite biodiversity—is a conceited notion put forward by our own foresters. We have lost over half of our recorded natural forests in a little less than 40 years of freedom.

If the attitude of the alien regime towards our forests was shortsighted, their attitude towards our wild denizens was, if anything, heartless. The East India Company's servants had the time of their lives hunting tigers and leopards, slaughtering them in hundreds. So casual had they become that they often did not even care to keep a count of the tigers they so wantonly killed. Judges generally do not have an outdoor career. Nevertheless, one civil judge bagged over 400 tigers in the short period of his service in Bengal. British soldiers, too, were keen hunters who hunted free style, block by block, for months. Indian royalty also indulged in hunting. Wild animals, including tigers, were notified as vermin and a bounty was paid if anyone was able to produce a tail or a head. In fact, even snow leopards continued to be branded as 'vermin' till the late 1960s.

But the trade in trophies and the tiger-hunting safaris that followed Independence were even worse than the earlier carnage. There is no reliable record of the resultant loss of wildlife, but it was enormous. With habitats destroyed, venison in the open market and skins available in bales for the fur trade, a lot was lost, bringing forty-two species onto the threatened list. Even the once common jackals became endangered.

Concern for nature conservation first began to build up in the early part of the present century, when Kaziranga became a sanctuary in 1911 and so did Manas in 1928. As a follow-up to the London Conservation Convention of 1933, Hailey National Park (now Corbett National Park) was established in the United Provinces (now Uttarakhand) in 1935. But many other wildlife areas were receiving partial protection as Reserved Forests or sanctuaries. In south India, Mudumalai Sanctuary dates back to 1938. By 1950, there were only 35 such Protected Areas with one national park, collectively extending over 5,490 sq km. In the early 1950s, there was a sudden awareness concerning wildlife conservation, largely among hunters who were discovering fewer victims for their guns. An Indian Board for Wildlife was constituted by the Government of India in 1952, and many states followed with State Boards for the same purpose. The driving force behind the Board was M.D. Chaturvedi, the first Indian Inspector-General of Forests. He was a keen hunter as were most of the other members. But at least they were genuine outdoor men who had some knowledge of wild animals, albeit acquired through the sights of their guns! Still, thanks to them, Shivpuri, Kanha and Tadoba could be declared national parks in 1955.

Wildlife conservation areas tripled by the end of the 1950s, but these were half-hearted and haphazard attempts at conservation. A few areas like Hazaribagh were named national parks without any legal support. Even those notified were not managed as national parks. A note in *With Gun and Rod in India*, published by the Government of India in 1956, is evidence in support. It records: 'In India, we follow the model set by the Hailey National Park in Uttar Pradesh where forest operations continue uninterrupted.' The only act prohibited was hunting. The subject was debated in every meeting of the Indian Board for Wildlife. I had the privilege of attending most of them till 1983 (soon after, the Board became virtually defunct, possibly on account of the tragic assassination of Mrs Indira Gandhi, prime minister of India, in 1984). The Board was confused and even recommended planting of fruit trees and agricultural crops for wild animals in the national parks. And it never objected to the carnival of 'live baiting' for tigers and lions. The national parks had no separate organisation of their own. The same forest staff that was in charge of supervising forest fellings was also supposed to protect the park, in addition to their other duties. The system ensured only the neglect of wildlife. Keen wildlifers or nature-loving foresters like F.W. Champion and A.J.W. Milroy had passed away and the voices of young foresters like us were easily ignored till we (along with other leaders, officials and conservationists like Dr Karan Singh, M.K. Ranjitsinh, Billy Arjan Singh) were called to a meeting with Mrs Gandhi on 10 September 1971 so she could establish for herself on how matters stood. The immediate outcome was 'The Wildlife (Protection) Act, 1972,' for which Dr Ranjitsinh worked hard in preparing the draft bill for the Indian Parliament. The Act of 1972 too would have remained another pious resolution if it had not been backed by special conservation measures such as Project Tiger, which was the culmination of a 15-year battle that I waged with like-minded people on the issue of banning tiger hunting. At the General Assembly meeting of the IUCN held at Delhi in 1969, my appeal that the Indian tiger was in danger since its numbers had fallen to less than 2,000 received overwhelming support. The debate climaxed with a rousing demand for a total ban on hunting tigers. The Indian tiger was listed in the Red Data book as a protected species and its hunting was finally banned in 1970.

The other concern was human disturbance. Even national parks were centres of grazing and logging. The project was conceived as an urgent ecological necessity to save the predator and its dwindling habitats in India. It was based on the sound scientific principle that no species can be saved in isolation. For the preservation of a species like the tiger—an apex predator of its biological pyramid—the natural balance of the entire ecosystem had to be ensured. Our approach was to cover a wide variety of biogeographic provinces that were representative of tiger habitats of India, and nine Tiger Reserves were established across the country.

The guiding principle of the project was to repose confidence in the power of recovery of nature. It was my privilege to execute the project as its founder-director. We were fortunate that the members of the first green brigade were all committed conservators.

No one in India raised any doubt or asked any questions about the strategy and we were able to proceed with the full support we needed, thanks to the leadership of Mrs Indira Gandhi and Dr Karan Singh. Project Tiger also received massive support from across the world. World Wildlife Fund, now known as World Wide Fund for Nature, donated a million dollars for the project.

Left to nature, habitats revived and improved, water regimes regenerated, prey populations increased and predator populations soon followed suit. Many species that had taken to a nocturnal way of life to avoid humans, returned to their natural diurnal ways, including the tiger. Wild animals, at least in the forests we were able to protect, shed their fear of man and roamed freely in their jungles.

In time, even experts from overseas who had initially criticised our 'trust nature to repair itself' strategy began to see that this was the right thing to do. The credibility and goodwill, both within India and from overseas, served to boost the morale of our field personnel even more and was a key factor in the success of the project. The tiger, our national animal, was on the way to being saved. What really established the future foundation for the tiger's survival was Prime Minister Indira Gandhi's very public message for Project Tiger, denouncing economic forestry. She wrote, 'Forestry practices, designed to squeeze the last rupee from our jungles, must be radically reoriented at least within our national parks and sanctuaries, and pre-eminently in our tiger reserves. The narrow outlook of the accountant must give way to a wider vision of recreational, educational and ecological value.' Later, she personally guided the project.

Project Tiger was heralded as the world's most successful conservation project of present times.

India had reason to be proud of.

But that was then.

Unfortunately, today, the forest department sits on heaps of their own failures, and if Project Tiger is a success, it is all too often in spite of the forest departments' apathy and not its willing cooperation. The question that looms over the future of wildlife is whether wildlife conservation can ever become a priority subject for India. With a population of 900 million, increasing at the rate of the whole Australian population each year, will there be any space left for wild animals? I believe the correct answer could be 'Yes.' This is because of the lingering endemic and developed culture of the people of India who still have compassion for their fellow-creatures and who hold nature in reverence. There are religious sects, like the Bishnois of western India, who have adopted certain animals like blackbuck and chinkara for preservation. Those that enjoy perpetual protection from man in the name of religion include monkeys, revered as the incarnation of Hanuman and allies of Lord Ram. Even the much hated rat is held sacred at the Karni temple in Bikaner, Rajasthan. Snakes are worshipped. Under Vaishnav and Jain influences, a large part of our population is vegetarian. All shooting and hunting of animals and birds covered in the list of protected species is banned throughout India. Law-abiding attitudes coupled with a respect for authority have also helped. But times have changed and conservation values have got discounted. Consequently, old mores are changing and forests and wildlife have been wiped out from many tracts. Our hopes rest only on the Protected Areas. Unfortunately, even they are replete with problems and their existence endangered.

Among the problems of our parks, poaching is a chronic one. It has exploded out of proportion in recent years. The trade in all parts of tigers, especially their bones for Chinese medicine is the new threat that is decimating the species. Similarly, rhino horn is the target. Both are traded as medicines, wines and aphrodisiacs by China, mainly to markets in Hong Kong, South Korea, Japan, Singapore, Thailand and the USA in thousands of cartons and bottles. According to a TRAFFIC 1994 report, China exported 40,900 kg and 3,514 cartons of medicines containing tiger derivatives in 1991. Though all the derivatives claimed may not be genuine, even a small fraction is enough to endanger our tigers and rhinos. Trade in other species like snow leopard, common leopard, all species of wild cats and even jackals is dangerous. One dealer disclosed to me his stock of 65,000 jackal skins in 1978, and I discovered 660 skins of foxes and dozens of desert cats at Jaisalmer. They were all ready to be dispatched to Pakistan for foreign markets. For every consignment we intercept, we must presume that much more escapes across the border to feed the trade. Rare birds, orchids and medicinal plants are also being smuggled out of the country posing threat to our rare flora and fauna. Since populations of endangered species are concentrated in our reserves, they are easily targetted, if our vigilance weakens. The Ministry of Environment is keeping a watch at the trade points and TRAFFIC India, which is a part of the WWF's TRAFFIC International, is doing a good job of tracing the sources of illegal trade. But that is all after the event. Much more is needed to keep our wildlife alive in our reserves. Unfortunately, because much of the trade and our failures are not subject to public scrutiny, the loss is generally hushed up.

Another huge threat comes from grazing by livestock—cattle, goats, sheep and camels—and I see no solution in sight. Grazing depletes the forage potential of a park; invites the hostility of herdsmen towards predators, and even grazers other than their own herds, creates tension, stresses and strains among the wild animals, forcing them to abandon their natural system of diurnal activity in favour of a nocturnal system. This unnatural change in behaviour brings about physiological changes in their mating systems, a lowering of their vitality and resistance to disease, and shortens their life-span. It also increases their vulnerability to predation. Domestic cattle are often carriers of communicable diseases to animals in the wild. They have been responsible for transmitting rinderpest to gaur, foot and mouth disease to deer, and anthrax to nilgai, sometimes resulting in entirely wiping out ungulates from parks.

A particularly lethal form of attack on forest habitats are the free axes of the unending trail of women bringing out head-loads of firewood out from parks, all said to be 'dry and fallen', but are not really so. This is serious, since we have already over-felled our forests and depleted wild habitats.

Attempts to save forests and wildlife often result in violent clashes and I have been witness to many horrors. The horrible stoning to death of a forester, the mysterious murder of Ranthambhore's Badhiya (the best field forest-guard I ever knew), the shooting of park guards at point-blank range, Fateh Singh's (the legendary director of Ranthambhore Tiger Project) head injuries and broken limbs and the fact that I had to defend Bhanwaria, my Kalighati companion, against a trumped-up charge of murder; such incidents make me sick. It is not easy to protect the forests and wildlife since the legal formalities of notification and proper demarcation on the ground of the areas to be protected have not been even initiated. Justice administered, if at all, is delayed and too lenient to have any deterrent effect.

The problem of villages inside the parks is our own creation. We brought them in to have ready and cheap labour at hand for forest cutting. Our 4,500-year-old history and our overpopulation have left no part of India free from man, not even remote forests. Poaching and ritualised killing of wild animals by tribal people continues to be a chronic problem. Earlier, when these people were few in number and killed only for food, they were a part of nature, as natural predators. But with the increase in population and commercial interest in venison, hides and bones, the killing of wild animals has become a business and a serious threat. Most forest villages are no longer small, and are now heavily consuming and exporting park resources, causing imbalances in the park systems. The best programme to restore the health of the parks is, of course, to relocate the villages outside the parks. In fact, the single programme that restored Ranthambhore and Kanha to their natural state was the shifting of the villages. Those who are arguing against resettlement on the grounds that the people affected are indigenous people who have as much right to live in the forests as the animals themselves are labouring under an erroneous notion that people actually can live next to wild animals in peace. Apart from this, those who claim and advocate human rights should also appreciate nature's rights, the rights of voiceless wildlife. They should understand that long before the 'indigenous' people or ecosystem people came in the scene, the habitat belonged to wild animals, birds and plants, exclusively and on priority. Our experience of relocation of people is that the operation is difficult, traumatic and, at times, when not carried out with sympathy and care, cruel. This is an operation which cannot be performed in an ad hoc manner; it needs a long time, sincere effort and a thorough understanding of the life of the people to be shifted. At the heart should be the acceptance that the lives of the people who shift should see a marked improvement. A national plan and the cooperation of political and social workers is essential to make a start and allow the process to develop on its own, with massive help from the government.

But there is no escape from, and no alternative to, shifting villages from the heart of the parks, at least from some parks, which should be re-designated for national conservation priority. I do not advocate that each and every present or future national park proposed be free from humans. This is impossible. But let us accept that the present man simply *cannot* live in close proximity with carnivores, or herbivores that eat their food crops. I, therefore, plead nature's freedom at least for those national priority Protected Areas to be called as 'National Wildlife Reserves'.

I can rightfully claim to have been a part of the management history of India's wildlife and national parks for nearly four decades and, therefore, I can confidently say that the single factor responsible for the present crisis of our parks is absence of a sound administrative system, a failure to develop professionalism and the lack of discipline in our conservation management.

In planning a defence strategy, the first requirement is the organisation of a body of qualified and committed defenders. Unfortunately, the proposal for creating a separate department to protect wildlife and manage parks and the organisation required for executing these tasks in the form of a specialised service still continues to be inconclusively debated. Each time it is our own foresters, by vociferous voice and vote, who have conspired to veto the proposal to set up a specialised service on the dubious pretext of its non-viability. Our pressing hard could get agreement only for the setting up of a 'Wildlife Wing', that too with its flight feathers clipped. The forest department takes all the decisions, whether of converting the best *shola* forests, the habitat of the endangered lion-tailed macaque, to tea or teak, or releasing vital parts of a park to marble mining. It has not been uncommon for the parks to be used as a dumping ground for unwanted personnel of the forest department, or as a sort of jail term without trial. In one park, the director was changed seven times in six years and a few appointed in 'purely' temporary capacity. I have yet to meet a park guard, a ranger, even an officer, who is not keen to revert to his forest department because of the step-motherly treatment meted out to those working for wildlife. At least, no one wants his link-line, of back and forth movement, to be blocked. Can we expect dedication and commitment for park management from such unwilling or half-willing, borrowed, dejected, rejected and above all, temporary personnel? No foundation can be laid on quicksand. The practice of such postings has not allowed park leadership, loyalty and scientific temper to develop and has lowered the prestige of the park management profession.

In the early 1980s, Mrs Indira Gandhi appointed a high-powered committee headed by the Vice-Chairman of the Planning

Commission to study whether wildlife and the parks could be placed under a functional department. On the committee's recommendation, the subject was identified as an independent discipline at the centre and a Central Wildlife Conservation Service was to be organised to support the proposed department. A pull-out from the Forest Service was planned but this time, a whisper-campaign by foresters confused the Vice-Chairman. At this crucial stage, what we needed was a whole-time, fully committed leader, like Stephen T. Mather, who established the National Park Service of the United States in 1916. Mather is remembered as a leader with 'inexhaustible steam and practical idealism of the livewire type' who effectively mounted a counter-attack on his counterpart, the Chief Forester of the US Forest Service, who was totally opposed to the creation of a National Park Service. A strikingly similar situation to our own! Then the Indira–Rajiv era of conservation ended. Our Mather is yet to be born!

In new India, several new departments have been raised with success to meet the specialised demands of law and order, like the Home Guards, Coast Guards and Border Security Force, and of scientific management in the areas of space, environment, telecommunication, radio and television and many more. It is a pity that Wildlife Reserve Management, which is a specialised job involving the scientific conservation of nature, still continues to be in the hands of woodcutters and exploiters and the proposed department is still being endlessly debated. An Indian Forest Service for Wildlife and Reserves is imperative with its own training programme.

It is already too late.

The parks should also look for more friends and partners. A national park is a public institution and should be open to auditors and critics, even to carping critics. It must be an open book. Non-governmental organisations can provide good expertise and extension services for awareness campaigns. They can create a more broad-based body of supporters, to share the parks' responsibilities and check on any aspect that might be getting neglected. But for Tarun Bharat Sangh of Alwar, Sariska would have been ripped open by the miners. It was the media, which brought to public view the plight of the tigers of Ranthambhore. Without this exposure, the tigers of Ranthambhore would have been wiped out under the dubious cover-up attempt of the state foresters, which helped the poachers rather than hindered them. We need NGOs to act as watchdogs of our national parks. They should all be partners in the park programme. Unless politicians, local people, students, researchers, scientists, journalists, visitors, everyone is concerned about the parks, the chances of their survival will be dim.

When I mention the involvement of the local people, I rule out their short-sighted 'appeasement' by way of concessions at the expense of the park resources on any account. There is no place for multiple utilitarian concepts of management under which forest operations can be allowed to continue uninterrupted in our parks. Project Tiger has demonstrated the ecological value of each of the species in the law of nature and of leaving nature undisturbed for achieving a natural balance in its ecosystem. Let our parks be conservation bastions to be preserved as the last strongholds of our natural ecosystem.

Unfortunately, India is now gripped in a dilemma—parks or people, and the latest, parks and people. The clamour for priority of millions of our people, who are struggling to procure even a single meal a day, over the protection of ecosystems is pushing our nature conservation programme into the background. The Protected Areas of our parks hardly exceed five percent of the total land area of India. If people cannot survive with 95 percent of our land area, how much is the addition of this tiny area going to help? Even if it does, for how many, and for how long, and at what cost?

All our Protected Areas are now threatened. Can we save them? Yes, only by a miracle, but this time one which can be brought about only by wide awareness and concern, strong political will, dedicated personnel and adequate funds. I repeat – dedicated personnel, not just more men. We also need adequate funds, *not* lavish grants. And, finally, a strong political will, as provided by Mrs Indira Gandhi, effectively demonstrated and practised, not clever declarations to be issued and filed.

My recollections of the deeply-dedicated forest guards sitting by the side of smouldering logs, telling me their stories, where I enjoyed their fathomless hospitality of dry chapatis and chillies pushed down with black tea, rekindle in me hopes of survival of my dreams since they are still realities for me. Dedication and determination backed by hard labour, bold and timely action, a strong hand (do not spare the gun and always support the guard), clear understanding and, above all, conservation consciousness among our people as part of our culture are needed to save the last remnants of India's pristine natural wonderlands and their wildlife.

Excerpted from *Lest We Forget*, Sanctuary Books, 2008

# Acknowledgements

Billy Arjan Singh. Legend, conservationist, philosopher, friend, guide. He passed away on 1 January 2010—and I imagine the forest and its denizens are in mourning, bereft at the loss of their strongest defender. I shall miss you so. I regret that he is not part of this book, even as he was, and still is , so intrinsic to India's wilds.

My thanks first to my publishers, Rupa & Co., who put forward the idea of this anthology.

I must express my deepest gratitude to the authors who generously contributed to the anthology—thanks for the faith (and for keeping deadlines, even when I didn't!).

Of particular note are Peter Jackson, Valmik Thapar, Ullas Karanth, AJT Johnsingh, Bittu Sahgal, Bikram Grewal, Shekar Dattatri, Bivash Pandav, Joanna Van Gruisen, Janaki Lenin—all of whom have aided me in my various wild quests, much beyond the scope of this book. Tom, my friend, thanks for your story, and even more, for Oakville.

Ranjit, I am thankful for your efforts in this quest. Hasmukh, Charudutt, Anindya, Theodore Baskaran—thanks for your gracious support. I am indebted to the photographers—who have always been generous with their work. I would especially like to thank Vivek Sinha, Kalyan Varma, Nanak Dhingra, Aditya Singh, Ramki Srinivasan, Jayanth Sharma, Niranjan Sant. My work would be so much poorer but for you.

My salute to the Late Krishna Narian, a keen wildlifer, who took the photograph of the Asiatic black bear in Dachigaam National Park. He is no longer with us, a huge loss to conservation.

A special thanks to the *Sanctuary Asia* family for throwing open their archives—and for permission to reprint articles from the magazine and Sanctuary Books.

Grateful acknowledgements—also from the publishers of this anthology—to the following publishers for permission to reprint material:

Harikrishnan & Penguin Books India for *Five Encounters* by M Krishnan from*Nature's Spokesperson.*

K. Ullas Karanth and *The Hindu Survey of the Environment* for *Recovering India's Wild Tigers*, and *Sanctuary Asia* for 'Saving the Indian Tiger'.

Valmik Thapar and Oxford University Press for *Day Eight* from*Ranthambhore: 10 Days in the Tiger Fortress.*

Theodore Baskaraṇ and *The Hindu* for *New Year at Gopalsamibetta.*

Ranjit Lal's article and Ravi Dayal Publishers for *A Pest is Born* from *Mostly Birds, Some Monkeys and a Pest.*

Amit Chaudhery and Banyan Books for *A letter to Teddy.*

Dhriti K. Lahiri-Choudhury and Permanent Black *for Gabbar Singh and Chomsky in Dalma*

Ruskin Bond for *The Leopard.*

*M,* and *Tehelka,* for *Red Cancer, Green Quarry.*

Thanks to James Champion and Amit Sankhala for access to the works of F W Champion and Kailash Sankhala.

I owe a debt of gratitude to Ashok Kumar, P K Sen, Fateh Singh. My thanks to all the forest officers and staff on the field who have helped me immensely in my task.

I would also like to thank Dr Rajesh Gopal, Ramesh Pandey, Susanta Nanda, S EH Kazmi, A Das, A N Prasad, Biswajit Mohanty and Aditya Panda for their help with my story.

My friends—always there, always supportive; some wild, the others who save me from lunacy: Meghna, Geeta, Gauri, Lauri, Joy, Bhavna, Urmila, Sandy, Malini, Rama, Mohit.

Thanks, Sheila masi, Rainy didi. Also, Aruna, Tejal and the rest of the gang.

Doginder, I think I did it—inspite of you and your evil designs to entice me away from work. Ditto Jimmyboy

A mere *thank you* is not adequate, nothing is, for my brother Jaspreet—who enables me to chase my dream, and fight my battles. Dad, thanks for being there, and believing in my cause.

And to Ma, to whom I owe *everything*.